Birds
by colour

To Paul Géroudet whose writing nourished and inspired my passion for birds,
and Philippe J. Dubois who, one day, showed me the way…

Birds
by colour

Marc Duquet

ILLUSTRATIONS BY

Alban Larousse

and **François Desbordes**

CHRISTOPHER HELM
LONDON

First published in Great Britain in 2008 by Christopher Helm,
an imprint of A&C Black Publishers Limited
38 Soho Square, London, W1D 3HB
www.acblack.com

ISBN: 978-0-7136-8994-5

Copyright © Minerva SA, Genève (Suisse), 1999, 2001
Copyright © Delachaux & Niestlé SA, Paris, 2007
Title of the original edition: Les oiseaux par la couleur
Published by Delachaux & Niestlé, Paris

A CIP Catalogue record for this book is available from the British Library.

This book is produced using paper that is made from wood grown in managed,
sustainable forests. It is natural, renewable and recyclable. The logging and
manufacturing processes conform to the environmental regulations of the country of origin.

Translated by Tony Williams
Commissioning Editor: Nigel Redman
Project Editor: Julie Bailey and Sophie Page
Edited by Marianne Taylor
Typeset by Julie Dando, Fluke Art
Cover designed by Terry Woodley

Printed in France by Pollina - n° L44802

10 9 8 7 6 5 4 3 2 1

Contents

Foreword

Whether illustrated with photographs or illustrations, guides to bird identification are numerous and bear witness to the general public's increasing interest in birds. However, very few guide books are specifically designed for the use of newcomers to birdwatching. It is easy for a beginner to get lost in a conventional field guide where species are ordered by their scientific relationships (taxonomy). Arranging species by their favourite haunts or habitats, as is the method of choice in some guides, is only useful up to a point, as birds are frequently observed outside their usual preferred habitat types, and very few are reliably restricted to a single habitat.

As birds' shapes and colours are their most immediately noticeable characteristics, we have chosen these criteria to lead the approach to bird identification in this guide. So in the Identification section (pp18–105) you will find all species with a red breast grouped together, all large dark water birds grouped together and so on, allowing easy comparison of species with similar characteristics whether they are closely related or not.

In the first part of the Identification Key a set of bird silhouettes is presented to enable you to narrow down your bird to a general group. From there you are guided to the members of that group in the Identification pages. The species are grouped by their prominent colour or colours, so for example the Great Tit appears on the page 'Birds with a Black Throat' but also on 'Birds with Green Upperparts' and so on. We have chosen drawings rather than photographs for this section so each species can be shown in an attitude and at an angle that highlights its distinctive features, allowing for easy identification.

The Species Accounts (pp106–199) are illustrated with photographs and give information on where, when and how to see each species – three questions in one which I have tried to answer by drawing on my experience in the field and the little tricks which can help to make every birdwatching outing a success.

This guide covers 184 of the more common species to be found in Britain and western Europe (France, Belgium, Spain, Italy, Germany and Switzerland).

Marc Duquet, January 2007

How to use this guide

This guide can be used in two ways: identifying a bird you have seen, and discovering how to find and watch species that you wish to see. The first part of the book deals with identification, while the second section presents an overview of where and how to observe each species – its habitat and distribution, and when and how to look for it.

IDENTIFYING BIRDS
Birds are an integral part of everyday life, they occur everywhere. There's no need to be a specialist to enjoy putting names to the birds you see, whether in the garden, in the street or out in the wider countryside. In this guide identification is tackled in two simple steps.

The identification key (pages 14 to 17)
First of all, from the 11 general bird silhouettes shown on page 14–15, find the one that most closely matches the shape of the bird you have seen. From here you are directed to pages of similarly shaped species (for example, waders with long bills and long legs). The last silhouette, of a typical 'little bird', is referenced to a supplementary diagram indicating the body part names used in the book. This allows you to narrow down your search further within this very large category by precisely placing the colours of your bird (red belly, grey back and so on). The identification keys relate directly to the true identification pages. These are grouped by colours and indicated by coloured corners (black, black and white, grey, brown, yellow, red, multicoloured). Species with multiple colours appear on several pages, so you can find the Goldfinch by any of its colours – red forehead, yellow wingbar and so on.

buzzard   gull   heron

partridge   robin

Identification pages (pages 18 to 105)
Birds with common characteristics are placed on a double page (general shape and colour for larger birds, colour of a body part for the smaller ones). The particular characteristics of each species are highlighted and indicated with an arrow and accompanying text. There are also supplementary notes on each species' preferred habitat and its general behaviour. On each double page a box includes species with more or less the same researched character (for example a grey back) that figure in another part of this guide. There's also a list of other species showing similar characters that are not included here; these can be found in conventional identification guides meant for more experienced observers (see 'Going Further', p218).

Generally speaking birds are depicted perched, however those species normally seen on the wing or that are more easily recognised by their shape and/or behaviour when flying are shown in flight as well (sometimes on a separate page along with other similar species).

Most are shown life size or smaller (size is given in the second part of the book) and species on the same page are rarely shown to the same scale (this is for technical reasons, for example when a very large bird shares the same character with a small species). However, relative size is always respected on each double page; small birds are always depicted smaller than larger ones.

The coloured corners allow easy access to the right illustrated pages without necessarily using the identification keys. Pages are grouped according to colour (for example, pages treating red-breasted birds are followed by those covering birds with red on the head). There is, of course, a great deal of tonal variation in bird colours as well as variation in individual interpretations of colour so, to simplify the process, the coloured corners indicate primary colours (for example, red corners cover birds with red, pink or orange characters).

OBSERVING BIRDS

Once a bird has been identified you may want to turn to the relevant page in the 'Species Accounts' section to learn more about it. These pages are arranged in systematic order (according to conventional scientific classification); an index (page 219) makes it easy to find any given species.

Goldfinch
Carduelis carduelis

The Goldfinch is an inhabitant of cultivated areas with bushes and hedgerows, of scrub and also large, well-wooded parks and gardens; common throughout Britain except in the far north, western islands and open upland areas. The colourful adults (male and female are very similar) are easy to identify; young birds don't have the adult's characteristic red face but do have the yellow wing-bars. It has a longish pointed bill used for extracting small seeds from wild plants, especially thistles and their relatives. It can also be attracted to gardens by cultivating suitable plants and letting them seed or by feeding *nyjer* seed (advertised as the 'Goldfinch magnet').

- **Length** : 11.5–12.5 cm
- **Food** : small seeds, insects
- **Clutch** : 5 eggs (March–July)

Linnet
Carduelis cannabina

With its bright pink breast and forehead the male is relatively easy to identify, the less distinctive, mainly brown and grey females and young can be much harder. This delightful little finch can be found throughout much of Britain, especially in areas of heath where gorse is abundant and along the coast; it also inhabits scrub and overgrown hedgerows. It is absent from much of northern Scotland and upland areas of England where to some extent it is replaced by the similar Twite. A resident, it forms flocks with other finch species outside the breeding season but unlike most hardly ever comes to gardens for food.

- **Length** : 13–14 cm
- **Weight** : 16–21 g
- **Food** : seeds, a few insects
- **Clutch** : 4-6 eggs (March–August)

Siskin
Carduelis spinus

This handsome little finch is becoming easier to see in the British Isles. It tends to breed in mature conifer forests and has increased with the increase in the area of Britain's mature conifer forests. During the breeding season it is commonest in the west and north, with outlying populations in the south in such places as the New Forest. It is more widespread in winter and may turn up wherever there are fruiting alders. Since the 1960s, it has also taken to visiting many gardens to feed on peanuts. Winter numbers are increased by birds arriving from the continent where it is quite widespread, especially in northern countries.

- **Length** : 11–12.5 cm
- **Weight** : 12–14 g
- **Food** : seeds, berries, insects
- **Clutch** : 3–5 eggs (March–July)

Crossbill
Loxia curvirostra

A species of conifer forests (especially where spruce trees are common), the Crossbill feeds almost exclusively on conifer seeds, extracting them from cones using its peculiar cross-tipped bill. A very localised species in Britain, it is usually difficult to find as it nearly always feeds high in the top of mature trees and changes breeding sites regularly. Numbers varying greatly according to food availability, there are occasional very good years following a large cone crop, when birds from the continent invade Britain. The almost identical Scottish Crossbill is the only species of bird found nowhere but Britain. It is found in the Scottish Highlands; an area that also has good numbers of the 'ordinary' Crossbill. In both species males are brick-red while females are dull green.

- **Length** : 16–17 cm
- **Weight** : 26–44 g
- **Food** : conifer seeds
- **Clutch** : 3–4 eggs (January–May)

194 | 196

Species accounts (pages 106 to 199)

This section includes various details of habits and habitat, an illustration and a photo for each species along with its English and *scientific* (in italics) names and details of size, weight, diet, breeding period and clutch size. A detailed text explains where, when and how to see the species, with information on preferred habitat and distribution within Britain and the near continent, including seasonal variations. There are also details of seasonal variations in numbers for resident species. For most species, practical information is given on how to find the bird, the result of the author's 30+ years of experience in observing birds in Europe.

There is a photo of each species, chosen for its aesthetic quality and showing the bird in its typical habitat (the photos show only wild birds in natural surroundings). Where possible birds aren't shown at the nest (photography at the nest may be a cause of breeding failures so we cannot encourage it). For some species the choice of photo has allowed us to show the species in a different attitude or plumage (female for example) than that depicted in the identification section.

ADDITIONAL INFORMATION (pages 200 to 218)
Supplementary pages at the back of the guide provide information on taking your interest in bird identification, observation and protection further:

• observing birds: advice on spending time watching and identifying birds in the wild (equipment, common techniques, most productive habitats)

• birds' colours: the most frequent variations of the primary colours seen in birds are discussed, along with frequently used terms (e.g. red, orange, pink, salmon-pink…)

• bird classification: how species are grouped scientifically, in what order the different families are arranged

• some ideas for attracting birds to your garden (winter feeding, providing nest boxes…)

• useful references and addresses: a list of the main bird protection societies in Britain and western Europe; a selection of references for further reading

Identification keys

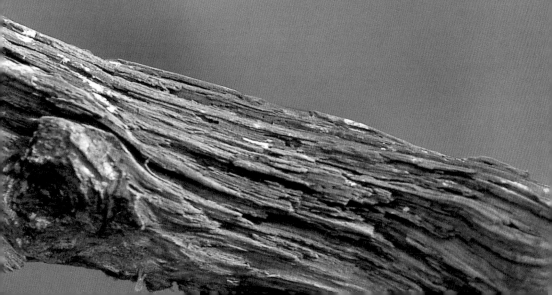

Identification key using silhouettes

Of the following bird silhouettes, choose the one that most resembles the bird you're trying to identify and go to the indicated identification page/pages.

■ Was the bird big with long neck and legs, like a heron or stork?

♦ Large birds with long legs (pages 34 and 36)

♦ Large birds with long legs, in flight (page 38)

■ Was it soaring in the sky like a buzzard or eagle?

♦ Birds of prey in flight (page 84)

■ Was it swimming like a duck?

♦ Black or dark water birds (pages 20 and 22)

♦ Large water birds in flight (page 40)

♦ White or colourful water birds (pages 98 and 100)

■ Was it a small or medium bird with long legs and/or a long bill, like a sandpiper?

♦ Small black-and-white waders (page 42)

♦ Small grey or brown waders (page 78)

■ Was it a stocky, round-bodied bird, like a moorhen or a partridge?

♦ Large birds of open country (page 74)

♦ Black or dark water birds (page 20)

■ **Was it grey and white, like a gull?**

♦ Large grey and white birds (pages 56 and 58)

■ **Did it look like a pigeon or a dove?**

♦ Large grey birds (page 54)

♦ Birds that are mainly brown or grey (page 70)

■ **Was it black all over, like a crow?**

♦ Entirely black birds (page 24)

■ **Was it a night bird, like an owl?**

♦ Nocturnal birds (page 76)

■ **Was it gripping a tree-trunk, like a woodpecker?**

♦ Spotted or striped and otherwise dull birds (page 82)

♦ Birds with red on the upperparts (page 94)

♦ Birds with red on the head (page 96)

■ **Was it small, the size of a sparrow or tit?**

♦ See the following page for a more refined search

Identification key using colour

This key covers the small and medium-sized land birds which have the classic and familiar 'generic bird' shape represented by the last silhouette on page 15. This is a very large group and includes birds such as sparrows, tits, finches and crows. This stage of the identification process works from the bird's overall colour or from at least one distinct coloured part.

General colour
First of all, consider the predominant general colour or pattern of the bird, whether it is uniformly plumaged or not.

* Entirely black birds (page 24)
* Black and white birds (pages 44 and 46)
* Birds typically looking black and white in flight (page 52)
* Birds largely grey or brown (pages 70 and 72)
* Dull, spotted or striped birds (pages 80 and 82)
* Multicoloured birds (page 102)
* Small birds which look multicoloured in flight (page 104)

Distinct areas of colour
If you have noticed distinct coloured patches or markings on the bird, use the diagram below to determine whereabouts the colour was on the bird's body. Although it's often unnecessary to use complicated plumage nomenclature, it will be helpful when using this guide to have an understanding of which general terms we have used to describe the various body parts.

Parts of a bird (Tree Sparrow)

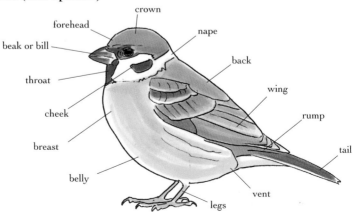

crown
forehead
beak or bill
nape
back
throat
wing
cheek
rump
breast
tail
belly
vent
legs

Illustrated index of the identification pages
The captions on the following illustration refer to the identification pages. The different colours that can be seen on the basic body parts are indicated; followed by the page number for birds showing that characteristic.

Head
- Black (pages 48 and 50) = birds with a black and white head
- Black and white (pages 48 and 50) = birds with a black and white head
- Grey (pages 66 and 68) = birds with a grey head
- Brown (pages 80 and 82 = dull, striped or spotted birds
- Chestnut (page 96) = birds with red on the head
- Pink (page 96) = birds with red on the head
- Red (page 96) = birds with red on the head
- Yellow (page 90) = birds with a yellow or green head
- Green (page 90) = birds with a yellow or green head
- Blue (page 102) = multicoloured birds

pperparts
- Black (pages 44 and 46) = black and white birds
- Grey (pages 60, 62 and 64) = birds with uniform grey upperparts
- Brown (pages 80 and 82) = dull, striped or spotted birds
- Red (page 64) = birds with uniform grey upperparts
- Green (page 88) = birds with green upperparts
- Blue (page 102) = multicoloured birds

Throat
- Black (pages 26 and 28) = Birds with a black throat

Cheek
- Black (pages 30 and 32) = birds with black on the cheeks
- White (pages 48 and 50) = birds with a black and white head
- Red (page 96) = birds with red on the head
- Yellow (page 90) = birds with a yellow or green head

nderparts
- Black (page 24) = entirely black birds
- White (pages 44 and 46) = black and white birds
- Brown (pages 80 and 82 = dull, striped or spotted birds
- Red (pages 92 and 94) = birds with red on the underparts
- Orange (pages 92, 94 and 102) = birds with red on the underparts; multicoloured birds
- Pink (pages 92 and 94) = birds with red on the underparts
- Yellow (page 86) = birds with yellow underparts
- Green (page 86) = birds with yellow underparts
- Blue (page 102) = multicoloured birds

Identification section

Black or dark water birds (1)

The way the bird positions itself in the water and its method of feeding may help in identification.

Yellow patch under the eye

No white on the throat

Head has curly crest in summer

White throat

Shag
Only on rocky coasts (Atlantic and Mediterranean). (p119)

Shag

Body mostly submerged whilst swimming

Cormorant

Cormorant
Coasts, also lakes, gravel pits and rivers (particularly in winter). Often in flocks. (p118)

Herring Gull (young)

Coasts and ports. Most young gulls have a similar plumage, lighter or darker depending on the species. (p143)

Plumage barred brown

Often feeds on dry ground

Moorhen

Moorhen

Rivers and lakes. Often hidden in waterside vegetation. (p133)

White bill and forehead shield

Red bill with a yellow tip

White bar under the tail

White line along the flanks

Entirely black body

Coot

Lakes and slow-flowing rivers. Often dives to feed. (p133)

Blue-grey bill

White body sides

Tufted Duck (male)

Lakes and slow-flowing rivers. Flocks, especially in winter. (p113)

Black or dark water birds (2)

Birds' colours and patterns often vary according to season, sex and age; young birds and females are often drabber than males.

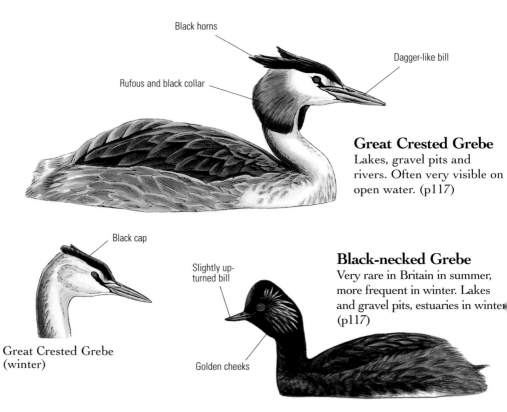

Black horns

Dagger-like bill

Rufous and black collar

Great Crested Grebe
Lakes, gravel pits and rivers. Often very visible on open water. (p117)

Black cap

Slightly up-turned bill

Black-necked Grebe
Very rare in Britain in summer, more frequent in winter. Lakes and gravel pits, estuaries in winter (p117)

Great Crested Grebe (winter)

Golden cheeks

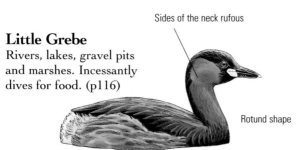

Sides of the neck rufous

Little Grebe
Rivers, lakes, gravel pits and marshes. Incessantly dives for food. (p116)

Rotund shape

> ➤ Similar species: Gadwall, Black-throated and Red-throated Divers, Common and Velvet Scoters, Slavonian and Red-necked Grebes, Ruddy Duck.

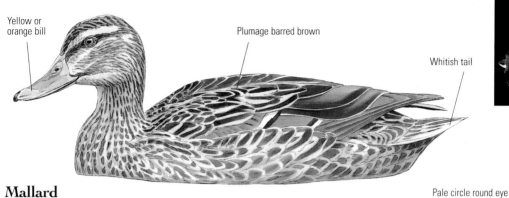

Yellow or orange bill

Plumage barred brown

Whitish tail

Mallard (female)
Lakes and rivers. Britain's commonest duck. (p110)

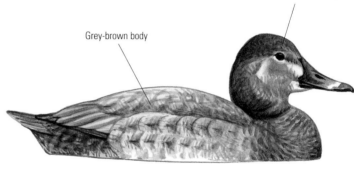

Pale circle round eye

Grey-brown body

Tufted Duck (female)
Lakes and rivers. Dives to feed. (p113)

Pochard (female)
More abundant in winter. Readily mixes with flocks of Tufted Duck. (p112)

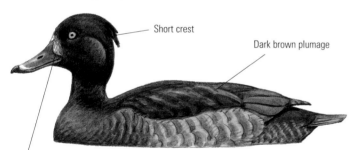

Short crest

Dark brown plumage

Sometimes has a little white around the base of the bill and/or under the tail

Teal (male)
All kinds of open water. The smallest European duck. (p110)

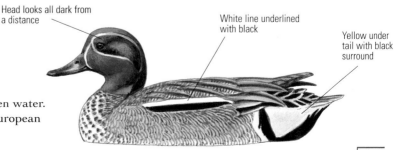

Head looks all dark from a distance

White line underlined with black

Yellow under tail with black surround

Entirely black birds

In the absence of any distinct coloured markings, it's important to note overall shape and the colour and shape of the bill.

Starling (spring)
Very common. Gathers in large flocks during autumn and winter. (p190)

Yellow bill

Body spotted cream

Spotless Starling (spring)
Mediterranean only (especially Corsica and Spain). (p190)

Shiny uniform black bo...

Yellow bill

Short tail

Grey nape

Whitish eye

Bright pink l...

Orange-yellow bill and ring around eye

Uniform black body

Longish tail

Blackbird (male)
Woodland, parks, gardens. (p168)

Pointed crown

White area at base of bill

Jackdaw
Tall buildings and cliffs. Often in flo... (p187)

Large bill

Diamond-shaped tail

Raven
Near mountains or coastal cliffs. Usually seen in pairs. (p189)

Rook
Nests colonially in trees (rookery). Flocks in fields. (p188)

Alpine Chough
Not found in Britain, common high in Alps and Pyrenees. Always in flocks. (p186)

ht yellow bill

Red legs

Chough
Rare. Coastal sites on west coast. (p187)

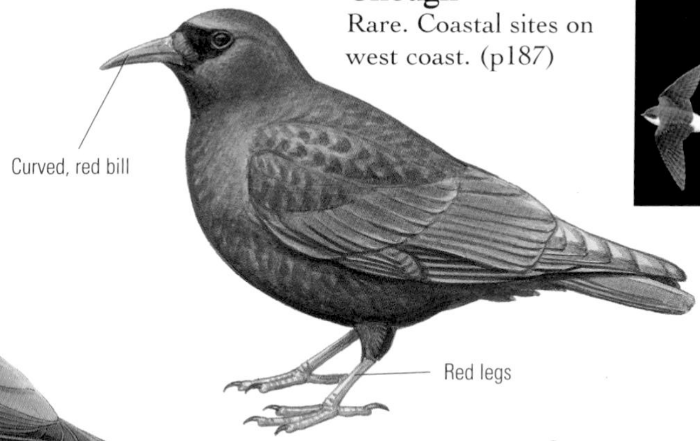

Curved, red bill

Red legs

Black bill

Rounded crown

Square-ended tail

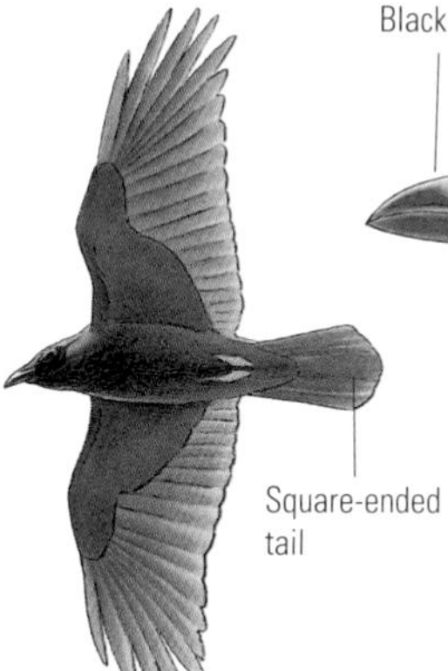

Carrion Crow
Common in towns and countryside. Usually seen singly or in pairs. (p188)

Black legs

Narrow, pointed wings

Short tail

Whitish throat

Swift
April to July. Does not perch, always seen in flight. (p152)

➤ See also: Black Redstart (page 61), Coot (page 21), Moorhen (page 21), Cormorant and Shag (page 20)
➤ Similar species: Black Woodpecker, Black Wheatear, Pallid Swift, Ring Ouzel, Blue Rock Thrush.

25

Birds
with a black throat (1)

Be sure to take note of the the extent and shape of any obvious coloured markings on the bird.

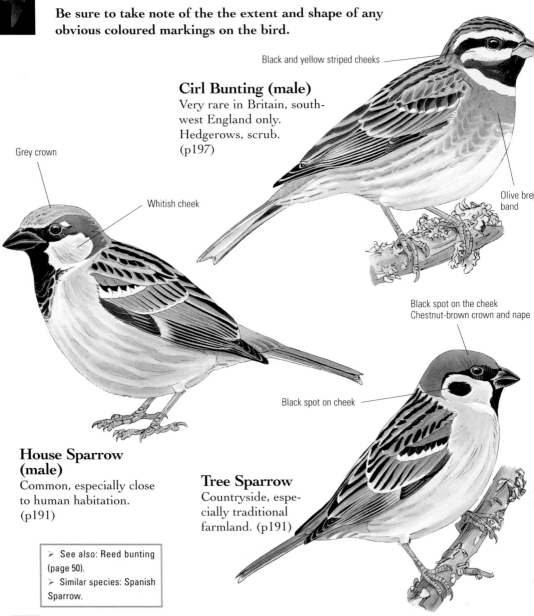

Black and yellow striped cheeks

Cirl Bunting (male)
Very rare in Britain, south-west England only. Hedgerows, scrub. (p197)

Grey crown

Whitish cheek

Olive breast band

Black spot on the cheek
Chestnut-brown crown and nape

Black spot on cheek

House Sparrow (male)
Common, especially close to human habitation. (p191)

Tree Sparrow
Countryside, especially traditional farmland. (p191)

> ➢ See also: Reed bunting (page 50).
> ➢ Similar species: Spanish Sparrow.

White mark on nape

Pale grey back

Coal Tit
Forests, especially
with conifers. (p179)

Beige underparts

Broad, clean
white cheek

Willow Tit
Deciduous woodland;
conifer forests at
altitude (continent).
(p178)

Pale bar along wing

Largish black bib
with diffused
edges

Pale brownish
flanks

White cheek

Green back

Black stripe down
belly

Yellow underparts

Great Tit
Very common everywhere:
woodland, hedgerows, parks
and gardens. (p179)

Pointed black-
and-white crest

Black pattern
on the cheek

Whitish cheek
with cream sides

Grey-brown
upperparts

Well defined
small black bib

eam underparts

Marsh Tit
Deciduous and mixed
woodland. (p178)

Crested Tit
In Britain only in Scottish
conifer forests; widespread
on the continent. (p179)

Birds
with a black throat (2)

Note as much pattern detail as possible when observing
a bird – this will help make identification more certain.

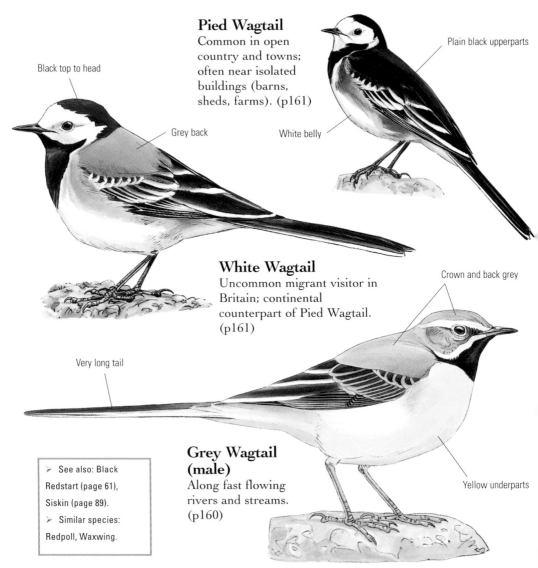

Pied Wagtail
Common in open
country and towns;
often near isolated
buildings (barns,
sheds, farms). (p161)

Plain black upperparts

Black top to head

Grey back

White belly

White Wagtail
Uncommon migrant visitor in
Britain; continental
counterpart of Pied Wagtail.
(p161)

Crown and back grey

Very long tail

Grey Wagtail (male)
Along fast flowing
rivers and streams.
(p160)

Yellow underparts

➢ See also: Black
Redstart (page 61),
Siskin (page 89).
➢ Similar species:
Redpoll, Waxwing.

All black head

Enormous conical bill

Large white mark in wing

Orange breast

Very short tail

Stonechat (male)
Meadows with scattered bushes, heathland. (p166)

Hawfinch
Uncommon in Britain. Deciduous woodland. (p196)

ale grey upperparts

Orange underparts

Ochre crown and back

All black wings

Orange tail

Whitish underparts

Redstart (male)
Open woodland, especially oak. (p165)

Black-eared Wheatear (male)
Not in Britain. Limestone plateaus and rocky slopes in southern Europe. (p167)

Birds with black on the cheek (1)

The time of year you see a bird may help identification. Some birds visit Britain only in the summer or winter.

Sky-blue wing patch

Jay
Large, shy woodland bird, most easily watched in autumn. (p185)

Pinkish underparts

Crown and nape chestnut-brown

Clean white cheek

Chestnut and black back

Yellow (or orange) crown

Large white 'eyebrow'

Tree Sparrow
Countryside with traditional farming, orchards and open woodland. (p191)

Firecrest
The smallest European bird. Rare in Britain. Bushes; deciduous and conifer woodland. (p176)

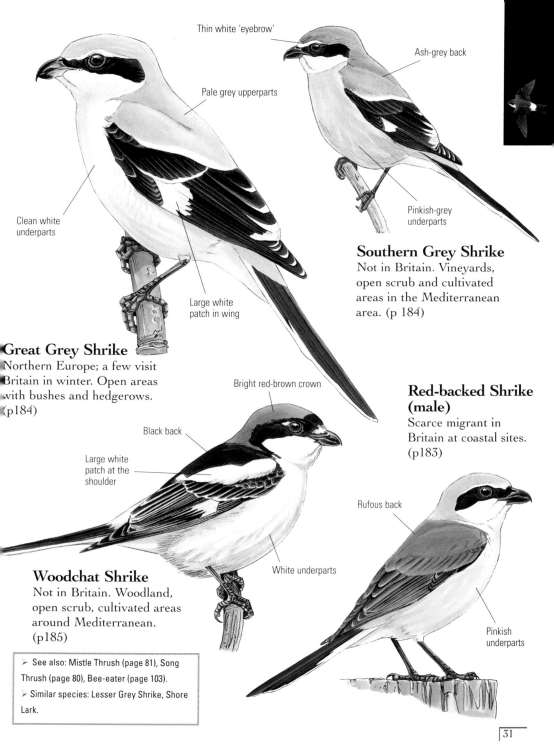

Thin white 'eyebrow'

Ash-grey back

Pale grey upperparts

Clean white underparts

Large white patch in wing

Pinkish-grey underparts

Southern Grey Shrike

Not in Britain. Vineyards, open scrub and cultivated areas in the Mediterranean area. (p 184)

Great Grey Shrike

Northern Europe; a few visit Britain in winter. Open areas with bushes and hedgerows. (p184)

Bright red-brown crown

Red-backed Shrike (male)

Scarce migrant in Britain at coastal sites. (p183)

Black back

Large white patch at the shoulder

White underparts

Rufous back

Woodchat Shrike

Not in Britain. Woodland, open scrub, cultivated areas around Mediterranean. (p185)

Pinkish underparts

> See also: Mistle Thrush (page 81), Song Thrush (page 80), Bee-eater (page 103).
> Similar species: Lesser Grey Shrike, Shore Lark.

Birds with black on the cheek (2)

With birds that have black on the cheek, it's important to see if the black covers the eye or extends to the bill or nape.

Black and yellow striped cheeks

Cirl Bunting (male)
Very rare in Britain, south-west England only. Hedgerows, scrub. (p197)

Black throat

Yellow underparts

Ochre crown and back

Black throat (sometimes white)

Whitish underparts

Black-eared Wheatear (male)
Not in Britain. Open rocky slopes in southern Europe. (p167)

Grey head striped black

Orange underparts

Rock Bunting
Not in Britain. Mountains, rocky coasts and scree in southern Europe. (p198)

➢ See also: Goldfinch (page 48), Whinchat (page 50), Redstart (page 61).
➢ Similar species: Penduline Tit, Bearded Tit.

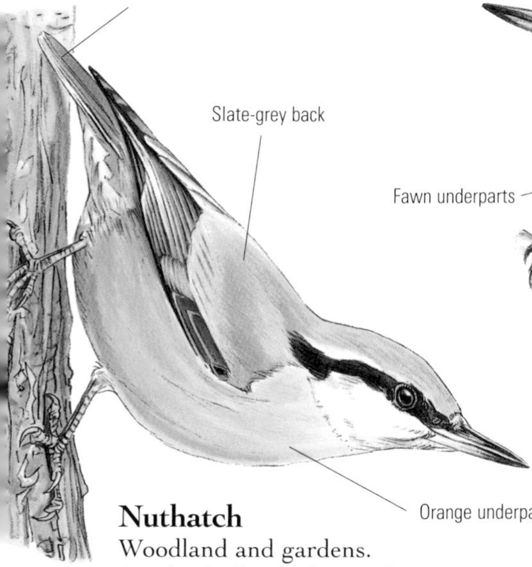

Short tail

Slate-grey back

Black top to head

Fawn underparts

Corsican Nuthatch
Found only in mountain forests on Corsica. (p181)

Orange underparts

Nuthatch
Woodland and gardens. Acrobatically climbs trunks and branches. (p181)

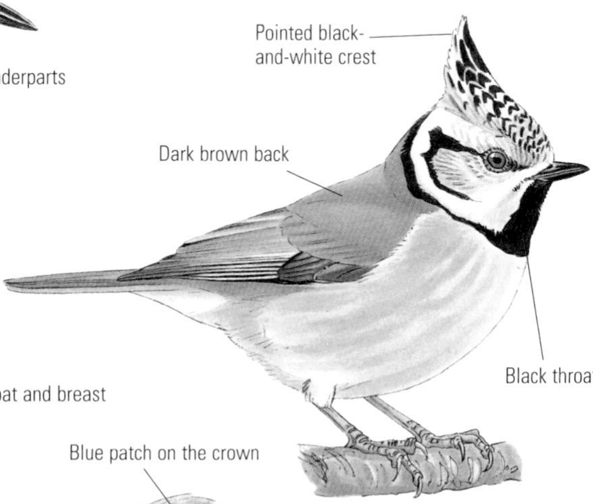

Pointed black-and-white crest

Dark brown back

Black throat

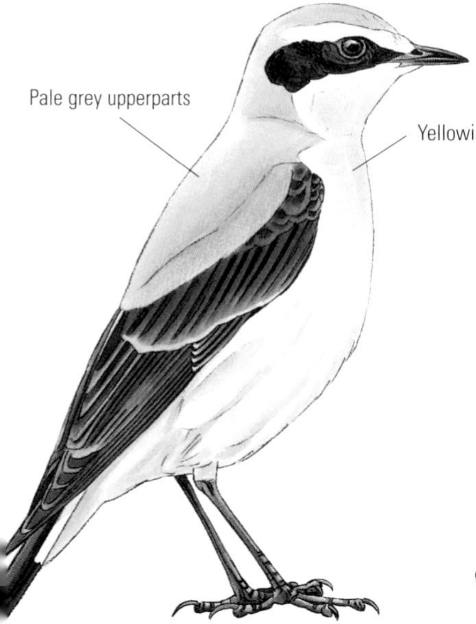

Pale grey upperparts

Yellowish throat and breast

Crested Tit
In Britain only in conifer forests in Scotland; widespread on the continent. (p179)

Blue patch on the crown

Blue Tit
Common wherever there are trees. (p180)

Yellow underparts

Blue wings

Wheatear (male)
Breeds in open country and uplands in the west and north of Britain. (p167)

Large birds with long legs (1)

Bill shape, colour and length are often important when identifying birds.

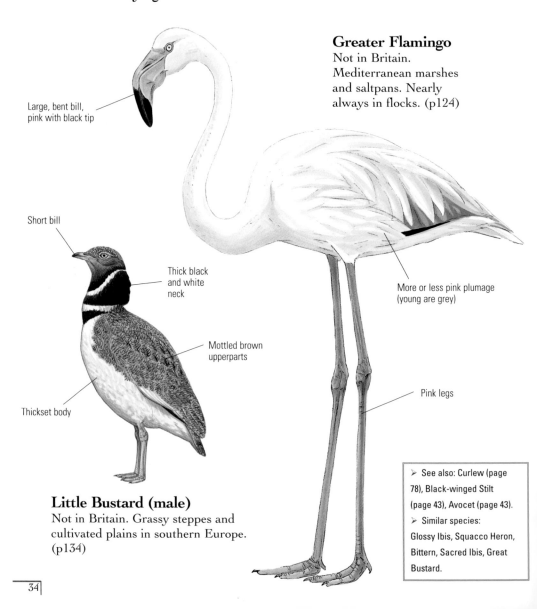

Greater Flamingo
Not in Britain.
Mediterranean marshes
and saltpans. Nearly
always in flocks. (p124)

Large, bent bill,
pink with black tip

Short bill

Thick black
and white
neck

Mottled brown
upperparts

More or less pink plumage
(young are grey)

Thickset body

Pink legs

Little Bustard (male)
Not in Britain. Grassy steppes and
cultivated plains in southern Europe.
(p134)

> See also: Curlew (page 78), Black-winged Stilt (page 43), Avocet (page 43).
> Similar species: Glossy Ibis, Squacco Heron, Bittern, Sacred Ibis, Great Bustard.

Quite short neck

Yellow or orange bill

Dark grey bill

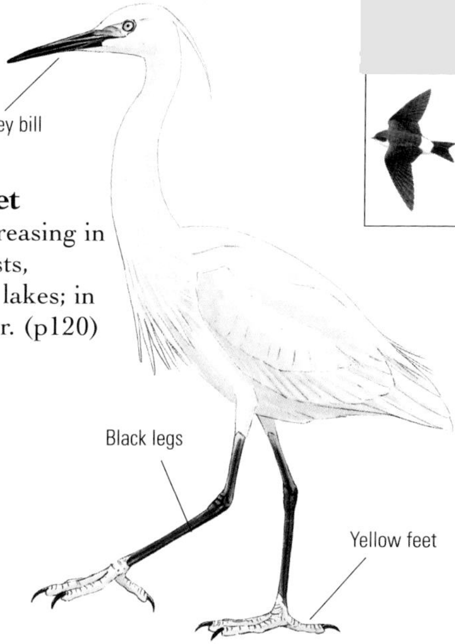

Little Egret

Rare but increasing in Britain. Coasts, marshes and lakes; in shallow water. (p120)

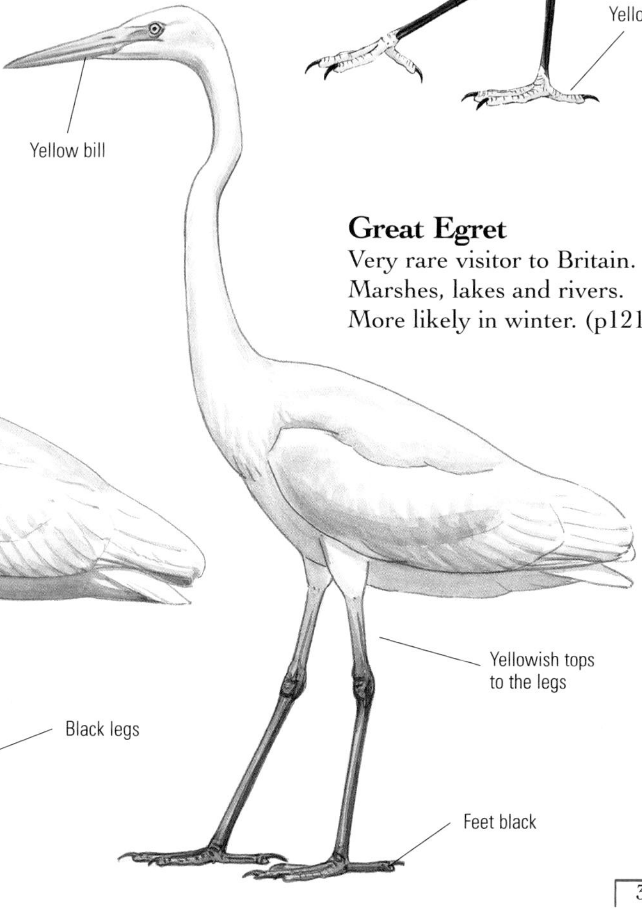

Cattle Egret

Not in Britain. Usually in flocks near livestock. (p120)

Black legs

Yellow feet

Yellow legs

ong, flattened bill

Yellow bill

Great Egret

Very rare visitor to Britain. Marshes, lakes and rivers. More likely in winter. (p121)

Spoonbill

Mudflats, estuaries and lakes. Passage migrant in south and east of Britain. (p123)

Black legs

Yellowish tops to the legs

Feet black

Large birds with long legs (2)

Note the exact position of any black markings: they can be decisive for identification.

White on side of head

Greyish yellow bill

Black neck

Black stripe on the head

Crane
Meadows and stubble. In Britain only a few pairs breed, all in East Anglia; commoner on the continent. (p134)

Orange-yellow bill

Grey underparts

Whitish underparts

Untidy tail

Grey Heron
Commonest tall bird. Rivers and lakes, also in meadows (especiall winter). (p121)

Night Heron
Not in Britain. Active at dusk and dawn, often perches in low, waterside trees. (p119)

Black bill

Black back

Red bill

Black neck and head

Black Stork
Not in Britain. Shy, forest species. (p122)

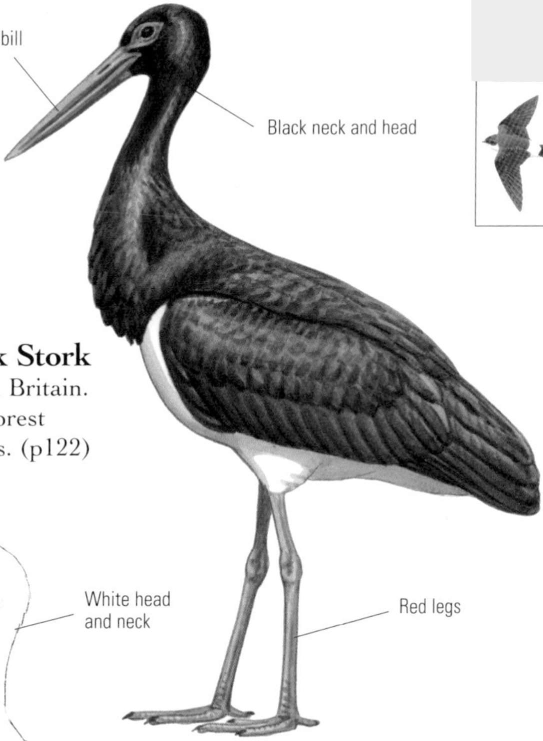

Red legs

Bright red bill

White head and neck

Black wings

Black streak on the cheek

Mostly brownish-grey with some reddish feathers

Red legs

Purple Heron
Very rare visitor to Britain. Reedbeds around lakes and ponds. Normally shy. (p122)

White Stork
Occasional in Britain. Marshes and meadows. Often perches and nests on high buildings. (p123)

Large birds with long legs, in flight

When colours can't be seen, the bill shape and positioning of the neck is often helpful for the identification of large birds in flight.

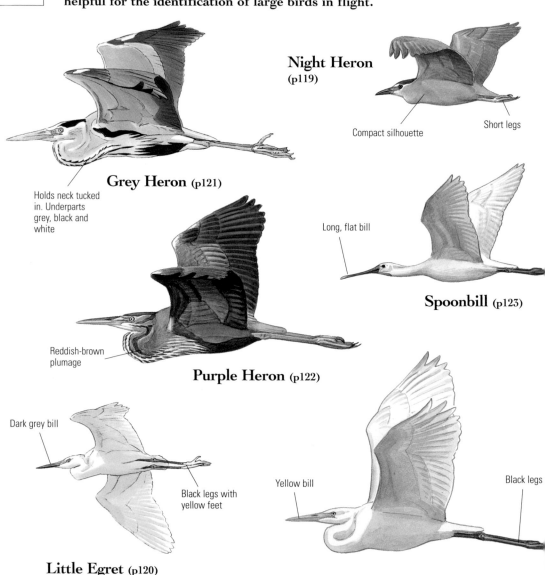

Night Heron (p119)

Compact silhouette

Short legs

Grey Heron (p121)

Holds neck tucked in. Underparts grey, black and white

Long, flat bill

Spoonbill (p123)

Reddish-brown plumage

Purple Heron (p122)

Dark grey bill

Black legs with yellow feet

Yellow bill

Black legs

Little Egret (p120)

Great Egret (p121)

Black wings

Greater Flamingo

Crane

Large white patch
on the belly

White Stork

Black Stork (p122)

Extended
neck

Crane (p134)

Red bill

White Stork (p123)

Wings black and
grey underneath

Black trailing
edge to wings

Black and pink wings

Long, drooping
neck

Very long legs

Greater Flamingo (p124)

Large water birds in flight

Flight speed and how fast the wings beat as well as wing shape are important clues for identifying flying birds.

Extended neck

Black plumage

Longish tail

Cormorant
Lakes, gravel pits
and coasts. (p118)

Greylag Goose
Fields, marshes,
coastal flats. (p108)

Short, pink legs

Cross-like silhouette

Cormorant

Very long neck

Mute Swan
Lakes, gravel pits
and rivers. (p108)

Short, black legs

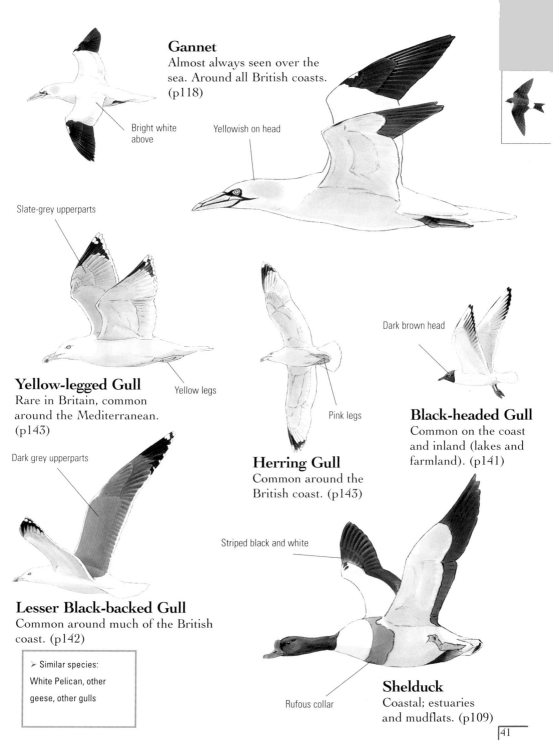

Gannet
Almost always seen over the sea. Around all British coasts. (p118)

Bright white above

Yellowish on head

Slate-grey upperparts

Yellow-legged Gull
Rare in Britain, common around the Mediterranean. (p143)

Yellow legs

Dark grey upperparts

Pink legs

Dark brown head

Herring Gull
Common around the British coast. (p143)

Black-headed Gull
Common on the coast and inland (lakes and farmland). (p141)

Lesser Black-backed Gull
Common around much of the British coast. (p142)

➤ Similar species:
White Pelican, other geese, other gulls

Striped black and white

Shelduck
Coastal; estuaries and mudflats. (p109)

Rufous collar

41

Small black and white waders

Small waders can often be identified by the length of their bill and legs. They are found on estuaries and sometimes muddy lake shores.

White wing-bar

Black bill

Narrow black collar

Orange and black bill

Plain brown wing

Largish black collar

Greenish legs

Little Ringed Plover
Gravel and sandy shores along rivers and by gravel pits. (p136)

Orange legs

Rufous vent

Long, slender, black crest

Ringed Plover
Mainly coastal (estuaries, mudflats, beaches) especially in winter. (p137)

Wide, rounded wings

Black bib

Lapwing
Marshes, meadows. Large flocks visit fields in winter. (p137)

> ➤ See also: Redshank (page 79), Common Sandpiper (page 79).
> ➤ Similar species: Kentish Plover, Ruff, Green Sandpiper.

Black-winged Stilt
Mainly Mediterranean, and occasionally occurs in Britain. (p135)

Straight, thin bill

Ungainly long pink legs

Solid black wings

Avocet
Scarce in Britain, mainly on south and east coasts, rare inland. (p136)

Upturned bill

Striped black and white above

Grey-blue legs

Oystercatcher
Estuaries and mudflats in winter, breeds in meadows in western and northern Britain. (p135)

Entirely black head

Long red bill

Short, pink legs

Large white wing-bar

Short tail

43

Black and white birds (1)

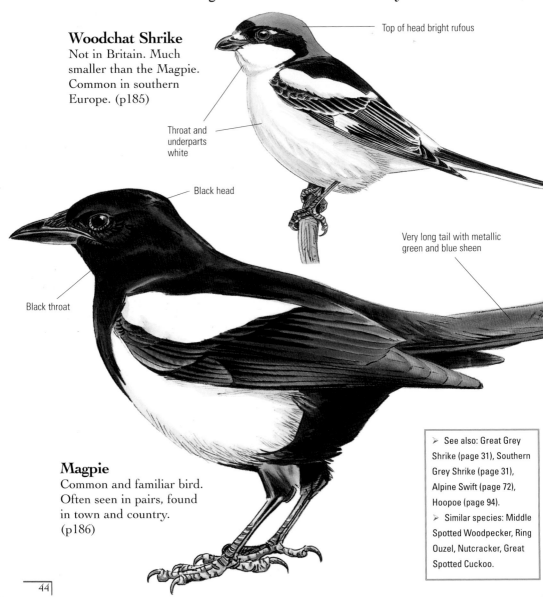

Choice of habitat often gives clues as to a bird's identity.

Woodchat Shrike
Not in Britain. Much smaller than the Magpie. Common in southern Europe. (p185)

Top of head bright rufous

Throat and underparts white

Black head

Very long tail with metallic green and blue sheen

Black throat

Magpie
Common and familiar bird. Often seen in pairs, found in town and country. (p186)

➤ See also: Great Grey Shrike (page 31), Southern Grey Shrike (page 31), Alpine Swift (page 72), Hoopoe (page 94).
➤ Similar species: Middle Spotted Woodpecker, Ring Ouzel, Nutcracker, Great Spotted Cuckoo.

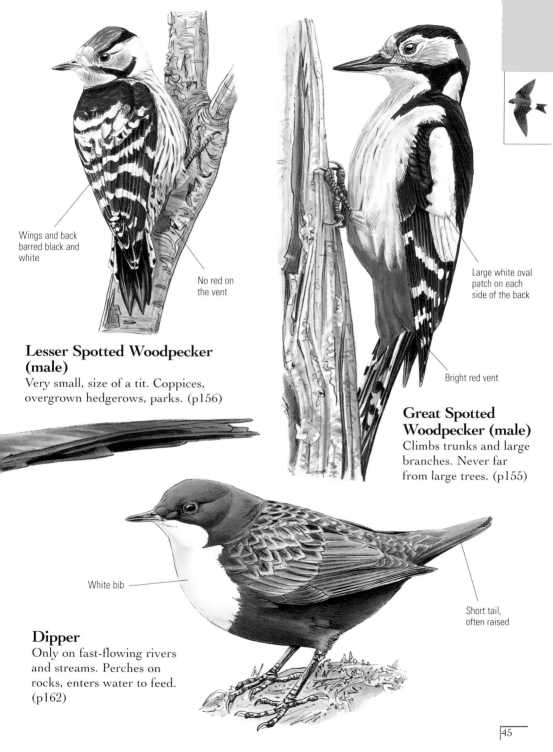

Wings and back
barred black and
white

No red on
the vent

Lesser Spotted Woodpecker (male)

Very small, size of a tit. Coppices,
overgrown hedgerows, parks. (p156)

Large white oval
patch on each
side of the back

Bright red vent

Great Spotted Woodpecker (male)

Climbs trunks and large
branches. Never far
from large trees. (p155)

White bib

Short tail,
often raised

Dipper

Only on fast-flowing rivers
and streams. Perches on
rocks, enters water to feed.
(p162)

Black and white birds (2)

The shape and length of the tail can be distinguishing features; remember to note them.

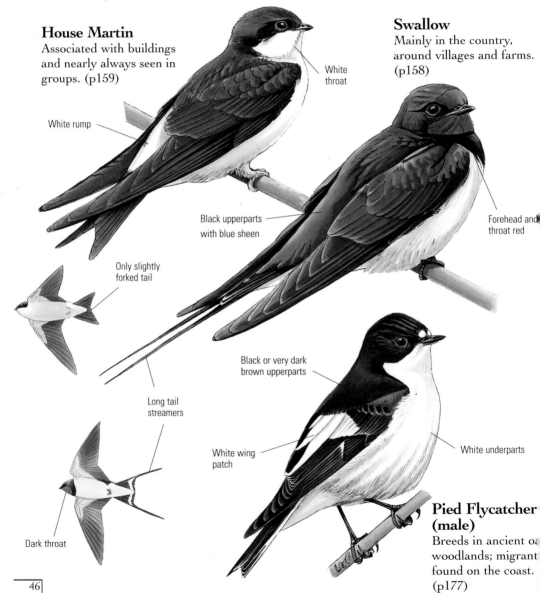

House Martin
Associated with buildings and nearly always seen in groups. (p159)

White rump

Only slightly forked tail

Black upperparts with blue sheen

White throat

Swallow
Mainly in the country, around villages and farms. (p158)

Forehead and throat red

Long tail streamers

Dark throat

Black or very dark brown upperparts

White wing patch

White underparts

Pied Flycatcher (male)
Breeds in ancient oak woodlands; migrant found on the coast. (p177)

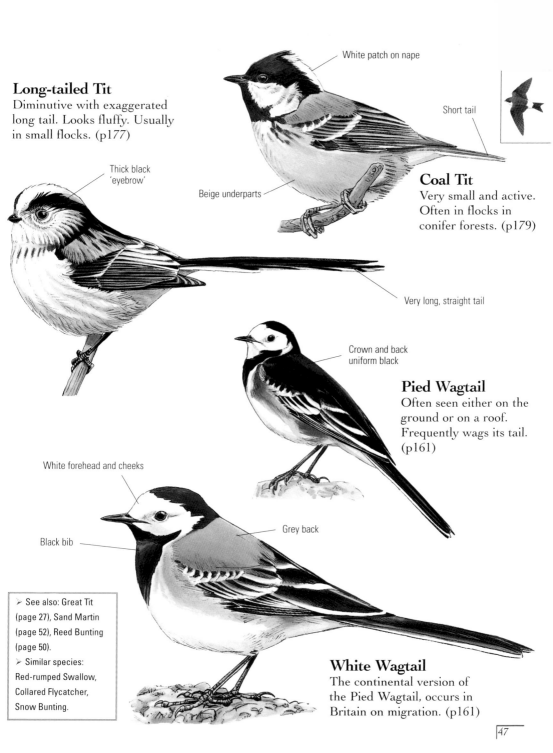

White patch on nape

Long-tailed Tit
Diminutive with exaggerated long tail. Looks fluffy. Usually in small flocks. (p177)

Short tail

Thick black 'eyebrow'

Beige underparts

Coal Tit
Very small and active. Often in flocks in conifer forests. (p179)

Very long, straight tail

Crown and back uniform black

Pied Wagtail
Often seen either on the ground or on a roof. Frequently wags its tail. (p161)

White forehead and cheeks

Black bib

Grey back

> See also: Great Tit (page 27), Sand Martin (page 52), Reed Bunting (page 50).
> Similar species: Red-rumped Swallow, Collared Flycatcher, Snow Bunting.

White Wagtail
The continental version of the Pied Wagtail, occurs in Britain on migration. (p161)

Birds with a black and white head (1)

When you're unsure about an identification, the most likely candidate in terms of habitat and date is usually the right one.

Uniform grey-brown wing

Marsh Tit
Deciduous and mixed woodland. (p178)

Cream underparts

Red face

Large yellow patch on the wing

Yellow (or orange) crown

Traces of yellow in the wing

Chestnut crown and nape

Goldfinch
Areas with numerous thistles, flocks in win (p194)

Back brown streaked black

Two narrow white wing bars

Firecrest
Rare in Britain. Tiny and very active. Bushes; deciduous and conifer woodland. (p176)

Tree Sparrow
Open countryside. (p191)

> ➤ See also: House Sparrow (page 26), woodpeckers (page 97).
> ➤ Similar species: PendulineTit, Rock Sparrow.

Pale grey back

Two narrow
white wing bars

Crested Tit
In Britain only in pine forests
in Scotland; widespread on
the continent. (p179)

Pointed crest

Back and wings
uniform brown

Coal Tit
Very small. In
conifer woodland.
(p179)

Beige
underparts

Green back

Whitish underparts

ack stripe down
lly

Yellow underparts

Great Tit
Very common. In wood-
land, hedgerows and
gardens. (p180)

Blue patch on the crown

Blue wings

Pale bar along wing

Largish black bib
with diffused
edges

Willow Tit
Deciduous woodland;
also conifer forests on
the continent. (p178)

Beige flanks

Blue tail

Blue Tit
Prefers higher branches
of trees; often in
reedbeds in winter.
(p180)

Birds with a black and white head (2)

Bad lighting (for example when looking into the sun) can distort colours. Take this into account when birdwatching.

Very long, straight tail

Tiny bill

Underparts washed pink

Long-tailed Tit
Resembles a ball of fluff with a very long tail. (p177)

Blackish back

Short tail

Orange breast

Whinchat (male)
Meadows and marshes with long grass. Chooses prominent perches. (p166)

Back brown with bold black stripes

White moustache

Belly streaked with black

Reed Bunting (male)
Wet ground with rushes, reeds and willows. Sparrow-like back. (p199)

Pied Wagtail
Often seen either on the ground or on a roof. Frequently wags its tail. (p161)

Back uniform black

Uniform grey back

Long tail

> See also: Stonechat (page 29), Goldfinch (page 48), Rock Bunting (page 32).
> Similar species: Collared Flycatcher, Lesser Grey Shrike.

White Wagtail
The continental version of the Pied Wagtail, occurs in Britain on migration. (p161)

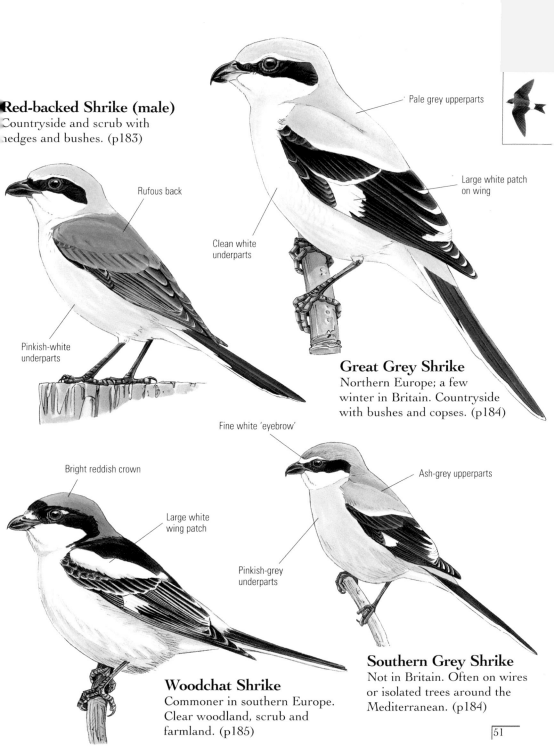

Red-backed Shrike (male)
Countryside and scrub with hedges and bushes. (p183)

Rufous back

Clean white underparts

Pinkish-white underparts

Pale grey upperparts

Large white patch on wing

Great Grey Shrike
Northern Europe; a few winter in Britain. Countryside with bushes and copses. (p184)

Bright reddish crown

Large white wing patch

Fine white 'eyebrow'

Ash-grey upperparts

Pinkish-grey underparts

Woodchat Shrike
Commoner in southern Europe. Clear woodland, scrub and farmland. (p185)

Southern Grey Shrike
Not in Britain. Often on wires or isolated trees around the Mediterranean. (p184)

Birds typically looking black and white in flight

Identifying birds in flight is not always easy – try to note
general colours, shape of wings and tail, and any calls heard.

Swift (p152)

Scythe-shaped wings

Black belly

Short, slightly forked tail

All black upperparts

White Wagtail (p161)

Triangular wings

Very long tail

Wheatear (male) (p1

White tail with
black band at end

Cream belly

Plain white
underparts

Uniform grey-bro
upperparts

Slightly forked tail

White belly

Deeply forked, long
tail

Dark collar

Slightly
tail

Swallow
(p158)

House Martin
(p159)

White rump

Sand Martin (p157)

Blackbird (male) (p168)

Long tail

Rounded wings

Jay (p185)

Triangular, pointed wings

Large white rump

White wing patch

Blue patches on the wing

Very short tail

Starling (p190)

Very long, tapering tail

➢ See also: Alpine Swift (page 72), Hoopoe (page 94).

➢ Similar species: Red-rumped Swallow, Snowfinch.

Magpie (p186)

White ends to the long wing feathers

Large grey birds

A bird's size can be estimated by comparing it to that of a familiar bird, such as a sparrow, blackbird or pigeon.

Rock Dove
The ancestor of the street pigeon – wild birds may still be found on remote northern coasts. (p146)

White rump

Red eye

Pale grey body

Two black wing bars

White patch on the neck

White wing bar

Woodpigeon
Larger than street pigeons. Common almost everywhere, including some cities. (p147)

> See also: Turtle Dove (page 71), Hooded Crow (page 73), gulls (page 56).
> Similar species: Great Spotted Cuckoo.

Black eye

Back same dark
grey as head

Stock Dove
Woodland and parks
with large trees.
Rare in towns.
(p147)

All grey plumage

Black wing bars
hardly visible

Black half-collar on nape

Uniform beige
upperparts

Collared Dove
Towns and villages,
farmland. (p148)

Broad white
bar at tail tip

Pinkish-cream
underparts

Long tail

Underparts
white, barred
with grey

Drooping wings

Cuckoo
Hawk-like summer visitor.
More often heard than seen.
(p149)

Large grey and white birds (1)

To identify gulls it's important to note the shade of the grey on the back and wings as well as bill and leg colour.

White patch in black wing tip

Common Gull

Wing tip entirely black

Kittiwake

Yellow bill

Yellow bill

Dark grey back

Kittiwake
Breeds on sea cliffs; winters at sea. (p144)

Black legs

Greenish-yellow legs

Yellow bill with red spot

Common Gull
Often seen inland; breeds in the north, winters every-where. (p142)

Pale blue-grey upperparts

Herring Gull
Common on nearly all coasts. Sometimes found inland. (p143)

Pink legs

Herring Gull

Yellow-legged Gull

Yellow bill
with red spot

Dark slate-grey
upperparts

Lesser Black-backed Gull

Breeds on many coasts,
often inland in winter.
(p142)

Yellow legs

Lesser Black-backed Gull

low bill
th red spot

Medium ash-grey
upperparts

ellow-legged Gull

ssentially Mediterranean;
ew occur in Britain.
143)

Yellow legs

Yellow bill with
red spot

Very dark grey-black
upperparts

Pink legs

Great Black-backed Gull

Huge gull, almost exclusively
coastal. (p144)

Large grey and white birds (2)

Some of the small gulls and terns have black on the head when breeding but not in winter; it's important to take season into account for a correct identification.

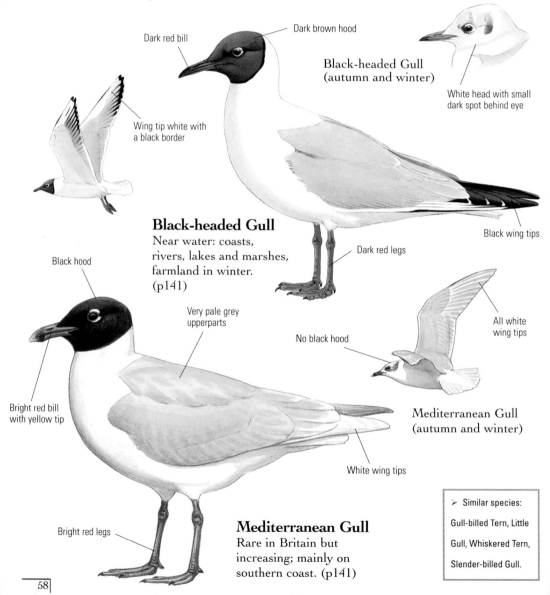

Dark red bill

Dark brown hood

Black-headed Gull
(autumn and winter)

White head with small dark spot behind eye

Wing tip white with a black border

Black-headed Gull
Near water: coasts, rivers, lakes and marshes, farmland in winter. (p141)

Dark red legs

Black wing tips

Black hood

Very pale grey upperparts

No black hood

All white wing tips

Bright red bill with yellow tip

Mediterranean Gull
(autumn and winter)

White wing tips

Bright red legs

Mediterranean Gull
Rare in Britain but increasing; mainly on southern coast. (p141)

➢ Similar species:
Gull-billed Tern, Little Gull, Whiskered Tern, Slender-billed Gull.

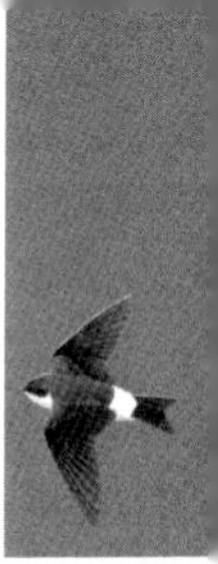

Black bill with
yellow tip

Shaggy nape

Sandwich Tern
Nests colonially on the coast,
quite scarce. (p146)

Slender, pointed wings

Short black legs

Rather short
forked tail

Sandwich Tern

Yellow bill tip often
invisible in flight

Black cap

Common Tern
Nests colonially inland and on
the coast. (p145)

Red bill with
black tip

Short, bright
red legs

Night Heron
Very rare visitor to Britain,
increasing on the continent.
Near water. (p119)

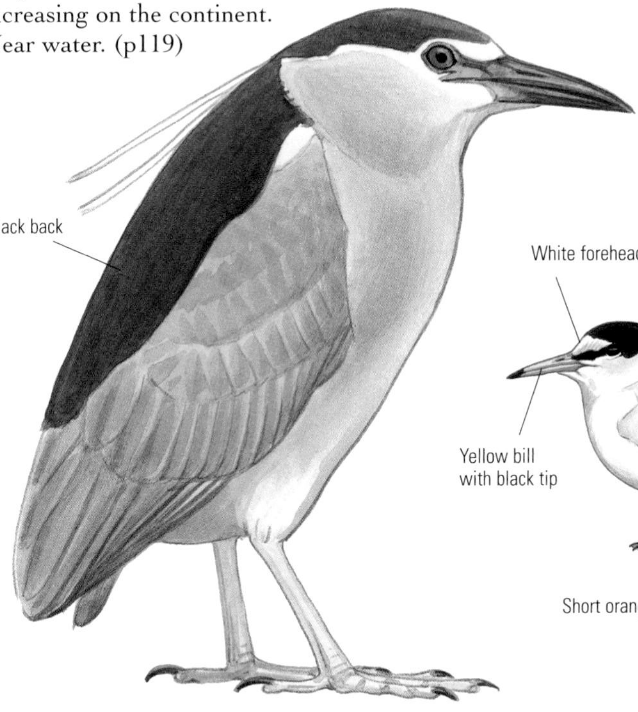

Black back

Wing shows black border

White forehead

Little Tern

Yellow bill
with black tip

Little Tern
Nests colonially on the
coast, often on beaches.
Rare. (p146)

Short orange legs

Birds with uniform grey upperparts (1)

When judging the tint of grey plumage, take account of the light. The same grey plumage looks darker in overcast weather than when it's sunny.

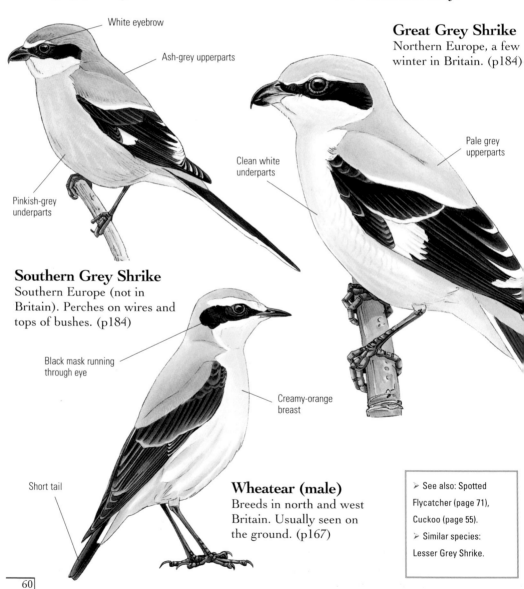

White eyebrow

Ash-grey upperparts

Pinkish-grey underparts

Great Grey Shrike
Northern Europe, a few winter in Britain. (p184)

Pale grey upperparts

Clean white underparts

Southern Grey Shrike
Southern Europe (not in Britain). Perches on wires and tops of bushes. (p184)

Black mask running through eye

Creamy-orange breast

Short tail

Wheatear (male)
Breeds in north and west Britain. Usually seen on the ground. (p167)

➢ See also: Spotted Flycatcher (page 71), Cuckoo (page 55).
➢ Similar species: Lesser Grey Shrike.

Redstart (male)
Open oak woodland, coastal scrub on migration. (p165)

Black throat

Orange underparts

Orange tail

Black Redstart (male)
Around buildings in a few areas of southern Britain. Quivers its tail. (p165)

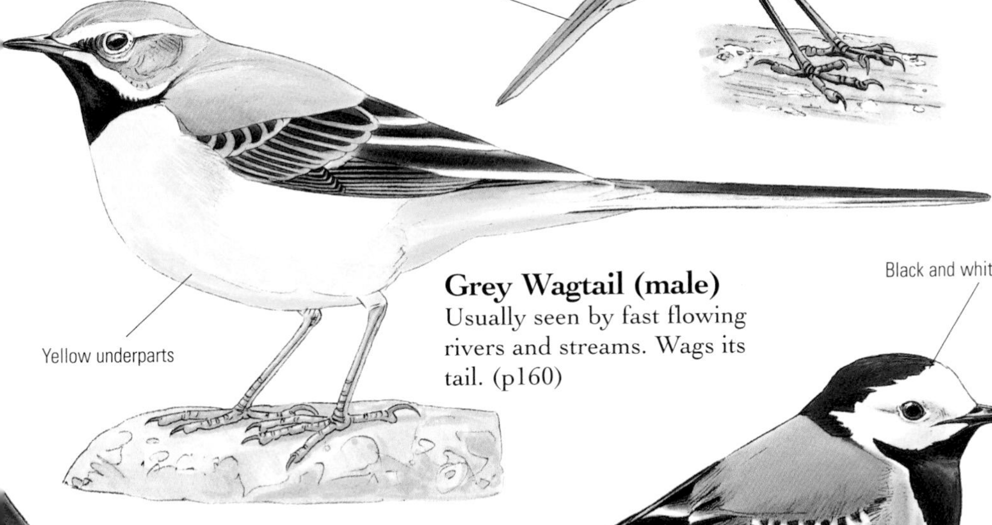

Grey-black underparts

Orange tail

Yellow underparts

Grey Wagtail (male)
Usually seen by fast flowing rivers and streams. Wags its tail. (p160)

Black and white head

White belly

White Wagtail (see also Pied Wagtail)
Uncommon visitor to Britain. Farmland and open countryside. (p161)

Birds with uniform grey upperparts (2)

Noting the way a bird moves (by walking or hopping) and where it perches can help you identify it.

Blackcap (male)
In trees and bushes.
Often hidden in the foliage.
(p174)

Well defined black cap (brown in female)

Black cap

Pale grey underparts

Fawn underparts

Corsican Nuthatch (male)
On Corsica only, in mountainous pine forests. (p181)

Black on head descends below eye

White 'eyebrow' and grey-blue crown

Bright red eye-ring

Sardinian Warbler (male)
Not in Britain.
Mediterranean scrub and gardens. (p172)

Whitish underparts

Corsican Nuthatch (female)

Red eye-ring

Short tail

White moustache

Brick-red underparts

Subalpine Warbler (male)

Not in Britain. Inhabits Mediterranean scrub. (p172)

Black eye-stripe

Rufous wing panel

White throat

Orange-brown underparts

Nuthatch

Runs up and down tree trunks and branches, often head-first. (p181)

Whitethroat (male)

Sunny, bushy places; often in hedgerows. (p173)

Quite uniform, no obvious markings

Garden Warbler

Woodland, copses and hedgerows. Normally stays hidden. (p173)

Birds with uniform grey upperparts (3)

Distinctive colours may be more or less visible according to the position of the bird. The longer you watch the bird the better the details can be seen.

White patch on nape

Two small white wing-bars

Fairly short tail

Black throat

Coal Tit
Usually in conifers, where it feeds acrobatically. (p179)

Shiny black cap

Uniform grey-brown upperparts

Small black bib

Dull black cap

Pale wing panel

Marsh Tit
Deciduous and mixed woodland. (p178)

Black bib with diffused margin

Willow Tit
Deciduous woodland and wet willow thickets. (p178)

> ➢ Similar species: Lesser Whitethroat, Dartford Warbler.

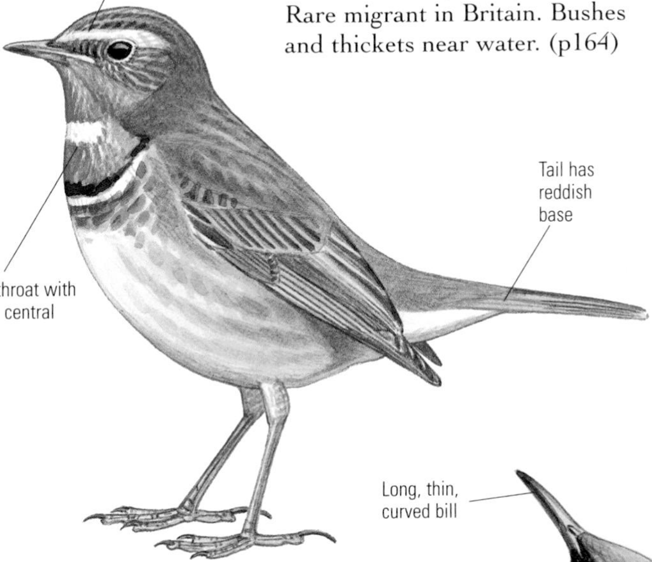

Pale 'eyebrow'

Bluethroat (male)
Rare migrant in Britain. Bushes and thickets near water. (p164)

Wide, round wings

Tail has reddish base

Blue throat with white central spot

Wallcreeper

Long, thin, curved bill

Black throat

Black cap

Blood-red wings

White wing-bar

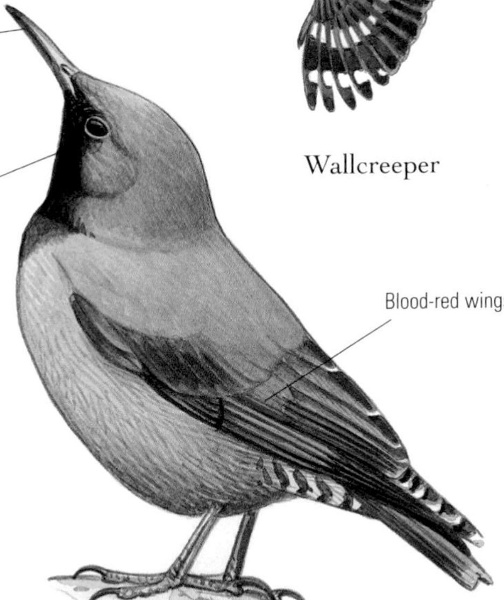

Wallcreeper (male)
Not in Britain. Climbs cliffs and vertical rock escarpments. (p182)

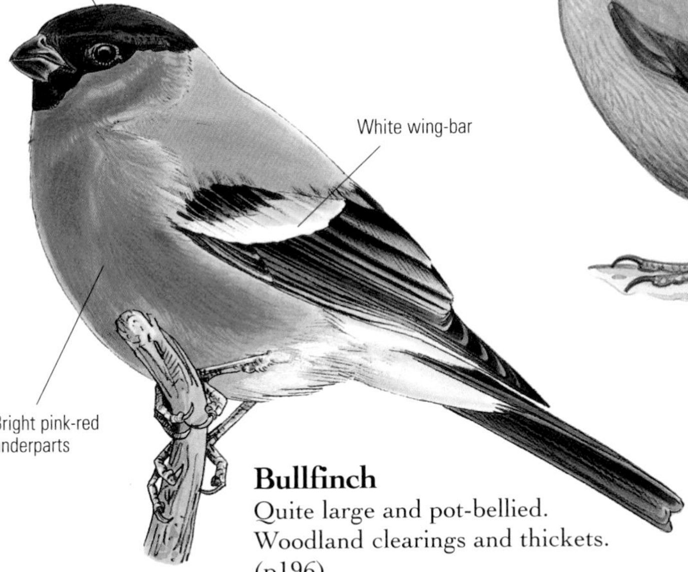

Bright pink-red underparts

Bullfinch
Quite large and pot-bellied. Woodland clearings and thickets. (p196)

Birds with a grey head (1)

Some species of bird are restricted to a certain habitat; others are more adaptable, or change habitat according to the season.

Conical bill

Whitish cheek

Black throat

Fine

Slate-grey underparts

House Sparrow (male)
Occurs wherever there are human habitations. At all altitudes. (p191)

Dunnock
Nearly always feeds on the ground, often under trees. (p163)

Rufous wing panel

White throat

Pinkish-cream underparts

Uniform grey upperparts

Black eye-stripe

Whitethroat (male)
Sunny, bushy places; rarely in large trees. (p173)

Nuthatch
Climbs tree trunks and branches. (p181)

Orange-brown underparts

Redstart (male)

Open woodland, coastal scrub when migrating. Quivers tail. (p165)

Black throat and cheeks

Orange underparts

Orange tail

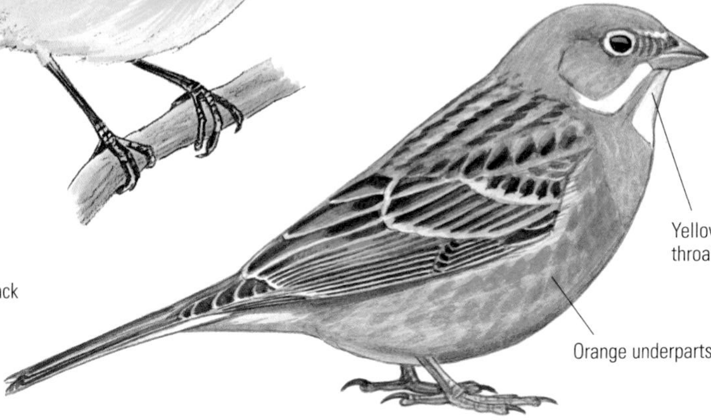

Bright red forehead

Chestnut back

Yellow throat

Orange underparts

Pink breast

Ortolan Bunting (male)

Very rare visitor to Britain. Rocky hillsides, vineyards in southern Europe. (p198)

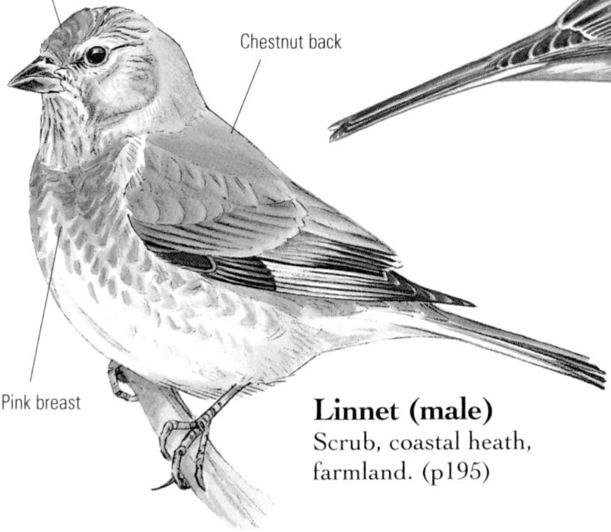

Linnet (male)

Scrub, coastal heath, farmland. (p195)

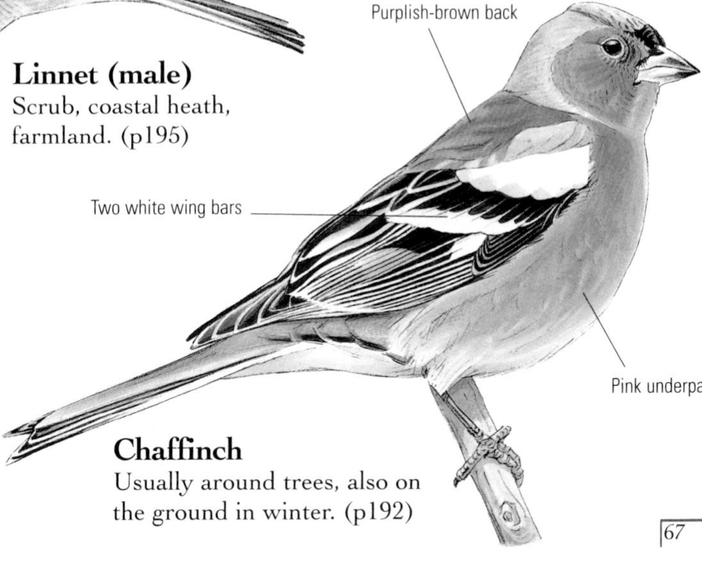

Purplish-brown back

Two white wing bars

Pink underparts

➢ See also: Subalpine Warbler (page 63), Brambling (page 93), Black Redstart (page 61). Similar species: Citril Finch, Snowfinch, Lesser White-throat, Alpine Accentor.

Chaffinch

Usually around trees, also on the ground in winter. (p192)

Birds
with a grey head (2)

Most birds have typical calls and songs, which are sufficient to identify a species, once you have learned them...

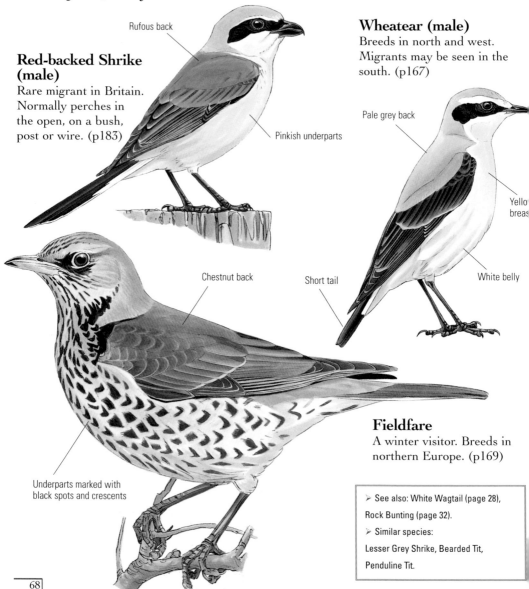

Rufous back

Red-backed Shrike (male)
Rare migrant in Britain. Normally perches in the open, on a bush, post or wire. (p183)

Pinkish underparts

Wheatear (male)
Breeds in north and west. Migrants may be seen in the south. (p167)

Pale grey back

Yellow breast

White belly

Chestnut back

Short tail

Underparts marked with black spots and crescents

Fieldfare
A winter visitor. Breeds in northern Europe. (p169)

> See also: White Wagtail (page 28), Rock Bunting (page 32).
> Similar species:
Lesser Grey Shrike, Bearded Tit, Penduline Tit.

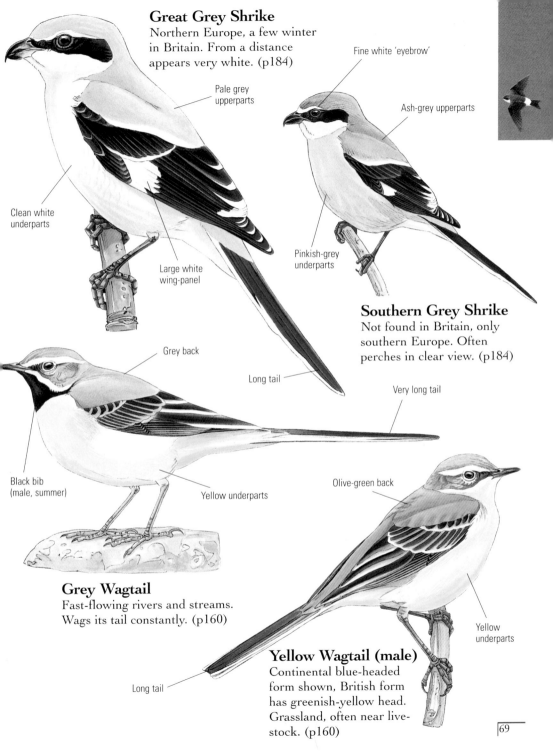

Great Grey Shrike
Northern Europe, a few winter in Britain. From a distance appears very white. (p184)

Pale grey upperparts

Clean white underparts

Large white wing-panel

Fine white 'eyebrow'

Ash-grey upperparts

Pinkish-grey underparts

Southern Grey Shrike
Not found in Britain, only southern Europe. Often perches in clear view. (p184)

Long tail

Very long tail

Grey back

Black bib (male, summer)

Yellow underparts

Grey Wagtail
Fast-flowing rivers and streams. Wags its tail constantly. (p160)

Long tail

Olive-green back

Yellow underparts

Yellow Wagtail (male)
Continental blue-headed form shown, British form has greenish-yellow head. Grassland, often near live-stock. (p160)

Birds that are mainly brown or grey (1)

Dull-coloured birds often have loud melodious songs that they deliver whilst hidden in foliage.

Nightingale
Scrub and bushes. Very secretive. In Britain southern England only. (p164)

Pale eye ring

Reddish tail, often cocked

Reed Warbler
Reedbeds and bushy marshes. April to October. (p171)

Cream 'eyebrow

Reddish rump

Elongated silhouette

Long white supercilium

Thick bill

White throat

Black and cream striped upperparts

Small cream wing-bar

Corscian Nuthatch (female)
Corsica only, in mountainous pine forests. (p181)

House Sparrow (female)
Towns and villages, at all altitudes. (p191)

Garden Warbler

Woodland, copses and
hedgerows. Rarely
shows itself. (p173)

No obvious markings

Long, thin,
curved bill

Black throat

Blood-red wings

Finely streaked head

Underparts
cream streaked
with grey

Wallcreeper (male)

Not in Britain. Mountains,
cliffs and vertical rock
faces. (p182)

Black and white
patch on neck

Wings rufous
spotted with
black

Spotted Flycatcher

Areas with scattered large trees
(parks, open woodland).
Perches in the open. (p176)

Turtle Dove

Arable areas with copses
and hedgerows. (p148)

Birds that are mainly brown or grey (2)

It is often difficult to define the colour of plain grey or brown birds, so be sure to note details of shape and any plumage contrast.

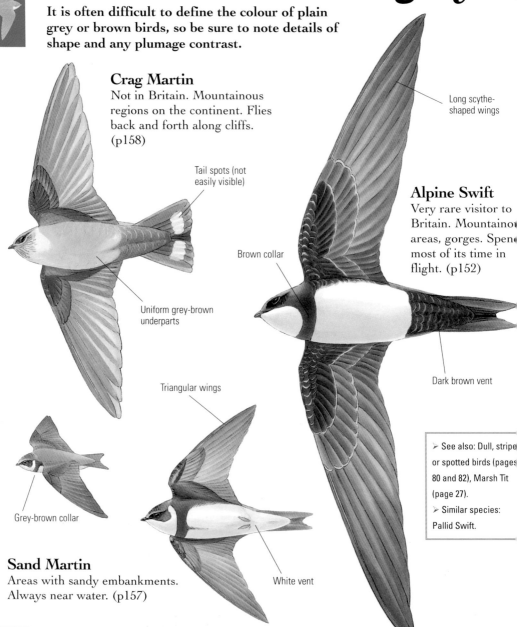

Crag Martin

Not in Britain. Mountainous regions on the continent. Flies back and forth along cliffs. (p158)

Long scythe-shaped wings

Tail spots (not easily visible)

Alpine Swift

Very rare visitor to Britain. Mountainou areas, gorges. Spen most of its time in flight. (p152)

Brown collar

Uniform grey-brown underparts

Dark brown vent

Triangular wings

> See also: Dull, stripe or spotted birds (pages 80 and 82), Marsh Tit (page 27).
> Similar species: Pallid Swift.

Grey-brown collar

Sand Martin

Areas with sandy embankments. Always near water. (p157)

White vent

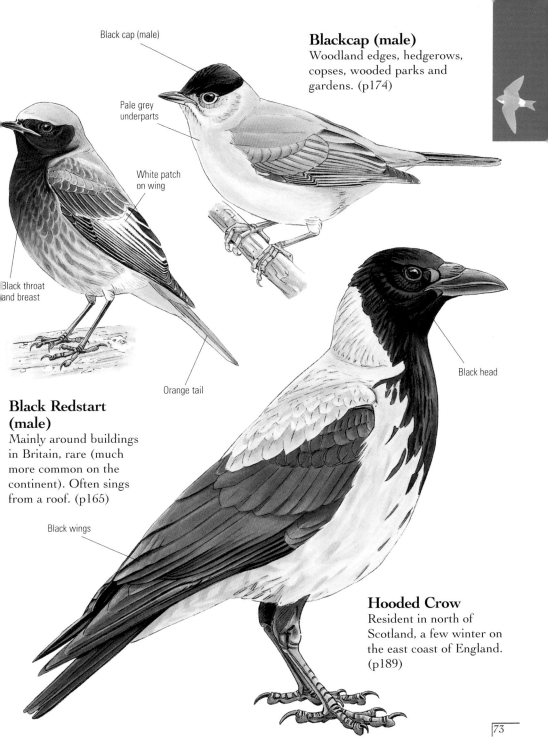

Black cap (male)

Blackcap (male)
Woodland edges, hedgerows, copses, wooded parks and gardens. (p174)

Pale grey underparts

White patch on wing

Black throat and breast

Black Redstart (male)
Mainly around buildings in Britain, rare (much more common on the continent). Often sings from a roof. (p165)

Black wings

Orange tail

Black head

Hooded Crow
Resident in north of Scotland, a few winter on the east coast of England. (p189)

Large birds of open country

Large ground birds are often wary; hiding or flying away when anyone approaches.

Very long down-curved bill

Very long down-curved bill

White lower back

Black neck

Quite long legs

White underpa

Curlew
Wet meadows and moors in summer, coastal mudflats in winter. (p139)

Quail
Very small. Hay meadows and crops. Rare in Britain, south only. (p115)

Dark throat

Short tail

Little Bustard (male)
Not in Britain. Meadows, crops and steppe on the continent. (p134)

Barred rump

Uniform grey rump

Grey Partridge
Mainly on arable land.
(p115)

Red-legged Partridge
Open country. (p114)

Striped back

Orange throat

White throat

Uniform back

Collar of
black spots

Black patch on belly

Chestnut barred flanks

Black and white
barred flanks

Bright red wattle

White wing

Pheasant (female)

Long pointed tail

Little Bustard

Long pointed tail

Pheasant (male)
Nearly everywhere on agricultural
land with hedges or copses; except
the far north. (p116)

> Similar species:
Corncrake, Stone
Curlew

Nocturnal birds

Seeing most owls and other night birds during the day is a matter of chance. At night they may be glimpsed in car headlights.

Short tufts

Scops Owl
Not in Britain. Villages, olive groves in Mediterranean. (p150)

Round hea

Large black eyes

Yellow eyes

Little Owl
Sometimes active in daylight. Orchards, cultivated areas. (p150)

Round head

White eyebrows

Black streaked underparts

White spots on underparts, becoming broader on belly

> Similar species: Eagle Owl, Short-eared Owl, Nightjar, Woodcock, Stone-curlew.

Tawny Owl
The commonest owl; but rarely seen. (p151)

Underparts streaked blackish-brown

Barn Owl

Long-eared Owl

Very prominent tufts

Clean white
underparts

Black comma
at 'elbow'

Orange eyes

ack eyes

Black-streaked
cream underparts

ite heart-
ped face

ite underparts
re or less
shed brownish

Upperparts
grey and gold

arn Owl
oosts and nests almost
clusively in roofs of old
rm buildings. (p149)

Long-eared Owl
Woods and copses. May
be seen on roadside posts.
(p151)

Grey or brown waders

Many waders migrate through western Europe in spring and autumn, mainly along the coasts. Most nest in the Arctic.

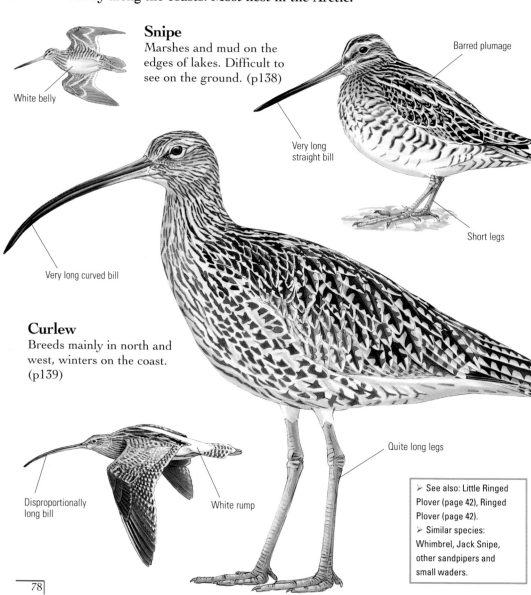

Snipe
Marshes and mud on the edges of lakes. Difficult to see on the ground. (p138)

White belly

Barred plumage

Very long straight bill

Short legs

Very long curved bill

Curlew
Breeds mainly in north and west, winters on the coast. (p139)

Disproportionally long bill

White rump

Quite long legs

> ➤ See also: Little Ringed Plover (page 42), Ringed Plover (page 42).
> ➤ Similar species: Whimbrel, Jack Snipe, other sandpipers and small waders.

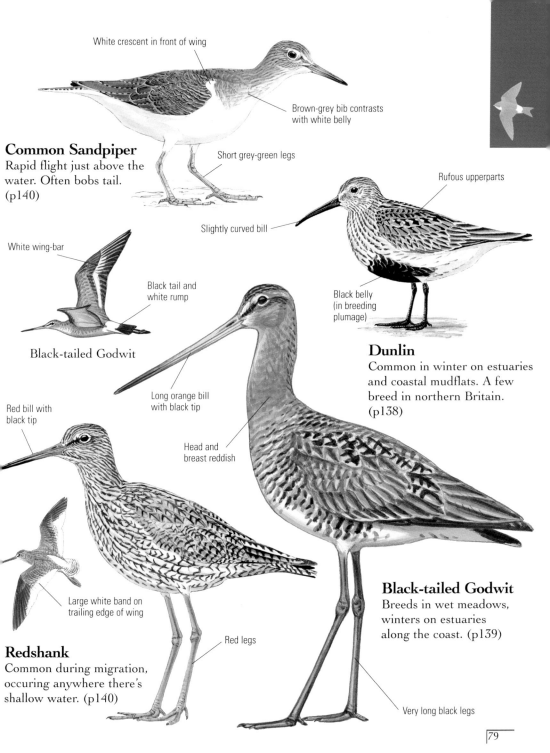

White crescent in front of wing

Brown-grey bib contrasts with white belly

Short grey-green legs

Common Sandpiper
Rapid flight just above the water. Often bobs tail. (p140)

Rufous upperparts

Slightly curved bill

Black belly (in breeding plumage)

Dunlin
Common in winter on estuaries and coastal mudflats. A few breed in northern Britain. (p138)

White wing-bar

Black tail and white rump

Black-tailed Godwit

Long orange bill with black tip

Head and breast reddish

Red bill with black tip

Large white band on trailing edge of wing

Red legs

Redshank
Common during migration, occuring anywhere there's shallow water. (p140)

Black-tailed Godwit
Breeds in wet meadows, winters on estuaries along the coast. (p139)

Very long black legs

Dull, striped or spotted birds (1)

Identification of 'little brown birds' often depends on observing their shape and behaviour. At a distance they can appear uniformly dark.

Fine bi[ll]

Brown and black streaked upperparts

White 'eyebrow'

Plain grey-brown back

Cream moustac[he]

Redwing
Winter visitor to Britain, in flocks with other thrushes. (p170)

Meadow Pipit
Wet meadows, heath, marshes, bogs. (p159)

Cream underparts streaked with

Underparts striped heavily with brown

Orange-red flanks

Olive-brown back

Grey head

Chestnut back

Black spots forming lines on underparts

Cream-washed brea[st]

Song Thrush
Woodland, parks an[d] gardens with trees. (p169)

Black spots and crescents on underparts

Fieldfare
Throughout Britain in winter. (p169)

> ➤ Similar species:
> Tree Pipit, Water Pipit,
> Rock Pipit, Alpine
> Accentor.

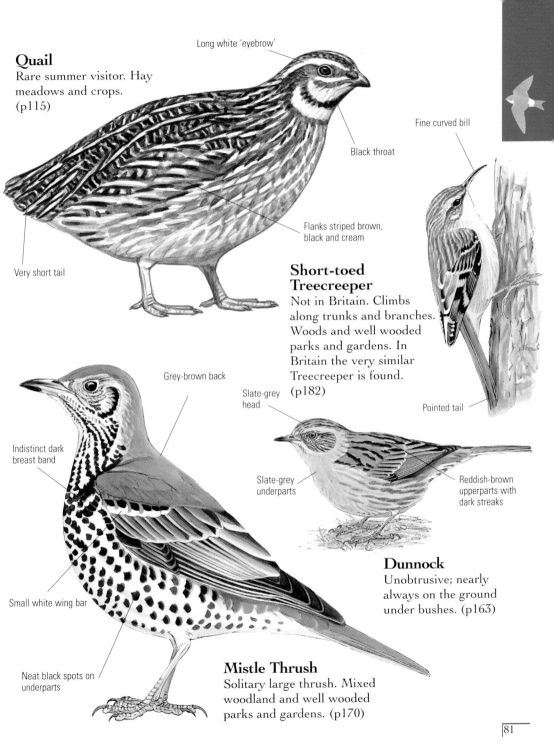

Quail
Rare summer visitor. Hay meadows and crops. (p115)

Long white 'eyebrow'

Black throat

Flanks striped brown, black and cream

Very short tail

Fine curved bill

Short-toed Treecreeper
Not in Britain. Climbs along trunks and branches. Woods and well wooded parks and gardens. In Britain the very similar Treecreeper is found. (p182)

Pointed tail

Grey-brown back

Slate-grey head

Indistinct dark breast band

Slate-grey underparts

Reddish-brown upperparts with dark streaks

Dunnock
Unobtrusive; nearly always on the ground under bushes. (p163)

Small white wing bar

Neat black spots on underparts

Mistle Thrush
Solitary large thrush. Mixed woodland and well wooded parks and gardens. (p170)

Dull, striped or spotted birds (2)

Whether they're in fields, under bushes or in trees, these birds' striped or spotted plumage is effective camouflage.

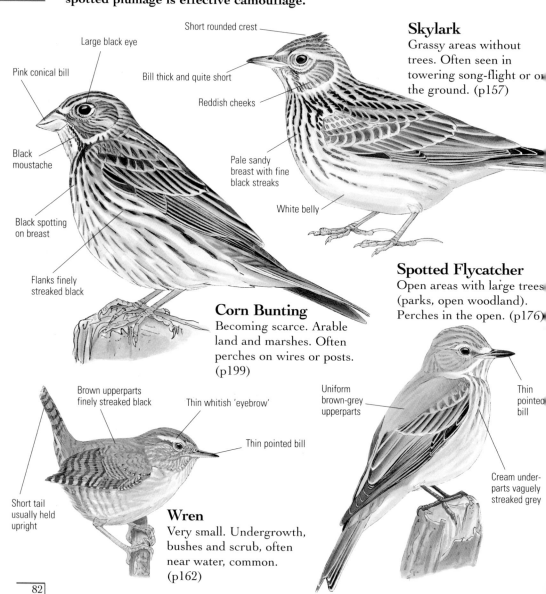

Short rounded crest

Large black eye

Pink conical bill

Bill thick and quite short

Reddish cheeks

Skylark
Grassy areas without trees. Often seen in towering song-flight or on the ground. (p157)

Black moustache

Pale sandy breast with fine black streaks

Black spotting on breast

White belly

Flanks finely streaked black

Spotted Flycatcher
Open areas with large trees (parks, open woodland). Perches in the open. (p176)

Corn Bunting
Becoming scarce. Arable land and marshes. Often perches on wires or posts. (p199)

Brown upperparts finely streaked black

Thin whitish 'eyebrow'

Uniform brown-grey upperparts

Thin pointed bill

Thin pointed bill

Short tail usually held upright

Cream underparts vaguely streaked grey

Wren
Very small. Undergrowth, bushes and scrub, often near water, common. (p162)

Long pointed crest

Finely striped brown-grey upperparts

Longish thick bill

Crested Lark
Not in Britain. All kinds of dry open areas on the continent. Usually seen on the ground. (p156)

Cream belly

Chestnut crown and nape

Black spot on cheek

Back chestnut streaked black

Uniform grey underparts

Grey crown

Whitish cheek

Black throat

Male

Tree Sparrow
Farmland and open countryside, often in flocks. (p191)

Buff 'eyebrow'

Quite strong conical bill

House Sparrow
Common wherever there are human habitations. (p191)

Vaguely streaked grey underparts

Female

➤ Similar species:
Woodlark, Rock Sparrow, Grasshopper Warbler.

Birds of prey in flight seen from below

To identify birds of prey in flight (often seen in silhouette) it's important to look for the precise shape and proportions of the wings and tail, as well as flight style.

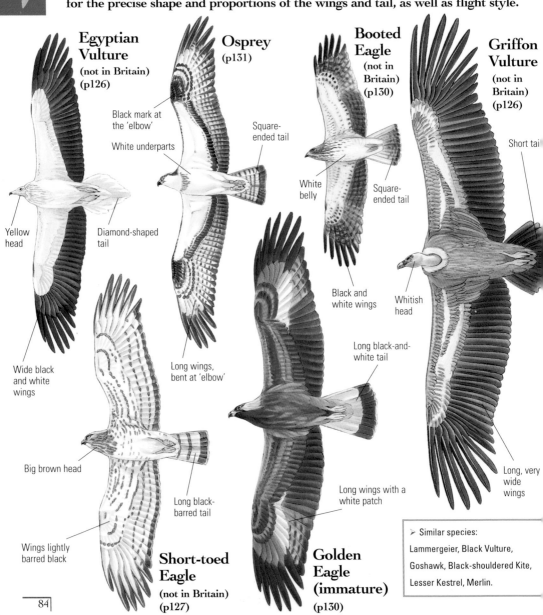

Egyptian Vulture
(not in Britain)
(p126)

- Yellow head
- Diamond-shaped tail
- Wide black and white wings

Osprey
(p131)

- Black mark at the 'elbow'
- White underparts
- Square-ended tail
- Long wings, bent at 'elbow'

Booted Eagle
(not in Britain)
(p130)

- White belly
- Square-ended tail
- Black and white wings

Griffon Vulture
(not in Britain)
(p126)

- Short tail
- Whitish head
- Long, very wide wings

Short-toed Eagle
(not in Britain)
(p127)

- Big brown head
- Long black-barred tail
- Wings lightly barred black

Golden Eagle
(immature)
(p130)

- Long black-and-white tail
- Long wings with a white patch

> ➤ Similar species:
> Lammergeier, Black Vulture,
> Goshawk, Black-shouldered Kite,
> Lesser Kestrel, Merlin.

84

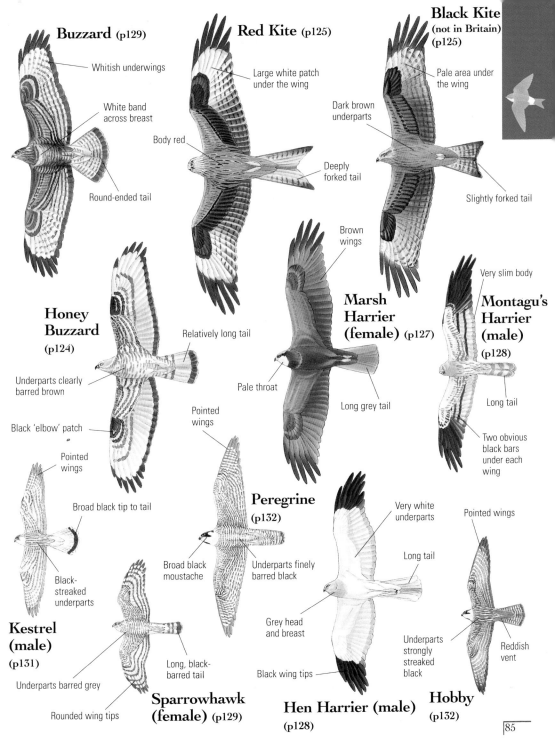

Buzzard (p129)

Whitish underwings

White band across breast

Round-ended tail

Red Kite (p125)

Large white patch under the wing

Body red

Deeply forked tail

Black Kite
(not in Britain)
(p125)

Pale area under the wing

Dark brown underparts

Slightly forked tail

Honey Buzzard
(p124)

Underparts clearly barred brown

Black 'elbow' patch

Pointed wings

Relatively long tail

Brown wings

Marsh Harrier (female) (p127)

Pale throat

Long grey tail

Montagu's Harrier (male)
(p128)

Very slim body

Long tail

Two obvious black bars under each wing

Pointed wings

Broad black tip to tail

Black-streaked underparts

Kestrel (male)
(p131)

Peregrine
(p132)

Broad black moustache

Underparts finely barred black

Long, black-barred tail

Underparts barred grey

Rounded wing tips

Sparrowhawk (female) (p129)

Very white underparts

Long tail

Grey head and breast

Underparts strongly streaked black

Black wing tips

Hen Harrier (male)
(p128)

Pointed wings

Reddish vent

Hobby
(p132)

85

Birds with yellow underparts

The dominant colour of a bird is rarely sufficient for its identification. Always look for additional characters (shape, colour, behaviour).

Blue cap

Black line through eye

Blue Tit
Common in woodland in the country and in towns (wooded parks, gardens). (p180)

Blue wings

Bright yellow head and back

Red bill

Golden Oriole (male)
Very rare in Brita[...] common on the continent. Poplar woodland. Difficu[...] to see. (p183)

Black crown, nape and throat

Green back

Black wings

Yellow-green upperparts

White cheeks

Greyish-green head

Yellow wing-bar

Great Tit
Often the commonest tit. Found almost anywhere there are trees. (p180)

Greenfinch (male)
Parks, gardens and hedgerows. Performs bat-like song-flight. (p193)

> ➤ See also: Siskin (page 89), Willow Warbler (page 89).
> ➤ Similar species: Citril Finch, Wood Warbler.

Cirl Bunting (male)

In Britain extreme south-west England only. Hedgerows, scrub. (p197)

Black and yellow striped cheeks

Black throat

Olive-green bib

Melodious Warbler

Very scarce migrant in Britain. Common hedgerow bird in southern Europe, April to September. (p171)

Slender orange bill

Grey-green upperparts

Pale yellow underparts

Yellow Wagtail (male)

Continental blue-headed form shown, British form has green/yellow head. Farmland, often near livestock. (p160)

Pale 'eyebrow'

Olive-green back

Yellow throat

Long tail

Yellow head

Chestnut rump

Rufous bib

Rufous-striped yellow underparts

Yellowhammer (male)

Countryside and arable areas. Stubble and ploughed fields in winter. (p197)

Entirely grey upperparts

Black throat

Very long tail

Grey Wagtail (male)

Nearly always along fast flowing rivers and streams. (p160)

Birds with green upperparts

In sunny weather, reflected light from green foliage can make birds look greener than they really are.

Small, thin bill

Indistinct cream 'eyebrow'

Bright red crown

Cream, sometimes slightly yellowish, underparts

Dark legs

Chiffchaff
Common summer visitor, a few overwinter. (p174)

Obvious yellowish 'eyebrow'

Willow Warbler
Common summer visitor in woodland. (p175)

Pale yellow belly

Pale legs

White cheeks

Yellow rump

Black stripe down belly

Great Tit
Very common: woodland, hedgerows, parks and gardens. (p180)

Yellow underparts

Green Woodpecker (male)
Open woodland, copses, orchards. Often feeds on ants on the ground. (p155)

Orange-yellow 'crest'

Black and white wings

White ring round eye

Goldcrest
Europe's smallest bird. Active. Woodland, especially conifers. (p175)

Orange or yellow 'crest'

Broad white 'eyebrow'

Black and white wings

Short tail

Firecrest
Rare in Britain. Bushes and conifers. Active and restless. (p176)

Black cap

Black and yellow wings

Yellow underparts

Siskin (male)
Commoner in winter; comes to bird tables. In flocks in stands of alder, willow or silver birch. (p194)

Grey-green head

Yellow wing-bar

Yellow-green underparts

Greenfinch(male)
Common. Parks, gardens and hedgerows. Flocks in winter. (p193)

Grey-blue head, yellowish-green in the British form

Yellow throat

Bright yellow underparts

Yellow Wagtail (male)
Blue-headed continental form shown (British form has green/yellow head. Grassy terrain, usually wet. Often in flocks. (p160)

Blue cap

Blue wings

Blue Tit
Common in woodland in the country or in town (wooded parks, gardens). (p180)

Long tail

> See also: Serin (page 91), Melodious Warbler (page 87).
> Similar species: Citril Finch, Grey-headed Woodpecker.

Birds with a yellow or green head

The shape of colourful markings on the tail or wings can help separate two species. Remember to look for them.

Yellow 'crest' with black edges

White ring round eye

Goldcrest
Tiny. In winter often joins mixed tit flocks. (p175)

Black and white wings

Broad white 'eyebrow'

Bronze sides of neck

Black eye-stripe

Firecrest
Rare in Britain. Bushes and conifers. (p176)

Yellow-green upperparts

Yellow wing-bar

Yellowish underparts

Greenfinch (male)
Common almost everywhere. Parks, gardens and hedgerows. (p193)

Obvious yellowish 'eyebrow'

Indistinct cream 'eyebrow'

Uniform olive-green back

Willow Warbler
Common summer visitor. (p175)

Pale yellow bel

Cream, sometimes slightly yellowish underparts

Pale legs

Dark legs

Chiffchaff
Common summer visitor, scarce in winter. Very active. (p174)

➢ See also: Golden Oriole (page 86).
➢ Similar species:
Wood Warbler, Citril Finch, Icterine Warbler, Shore Lark.

Black eye-stripe

Black throat

Yellow belly

Cirl Bunting (male)
In Britain only in extreme south-west England. Hedgerows, scrub. (p197)

Black cap

Green back

Black and yellow wings

Yellow under-parts, streaked black

Siskin
Commoner in winter; even comes to bird tables. Breeds in conifers. (p194)

Rufous bib

Rufous-striped yellow underparts

Chestnut rump

Yellowhammer (male)
Countryside, arable farmland. In flocks in winter. (p197)

Slender orange bill

Grey-green upperparts

Pale yellow underparts

Melodious Warbler
Very scarce migrant in Britain. Common hedgerow bird in southern Europe. (p171)

Green, striped upperparts

Tiny conical bill

Yellow breast

Black-striped white vent

Serin (male)
Rare visitor to Britain; common summer visitor to parks and large gardens on the continent. (p193)

Birds with red on the underparts (1)

Many birds have some shade of red, pink or orange in their plumage – as it's difficult to define the exact colour, all are treated here.

Black head

Stonechat (male)
Bushy waste and scrub. Often selects a prominent perch on a post or the top of a bush. (p166)

Black upperparts

White patch on neck

Short tail

Grey head

Bright red forehead

Chestnut back

Linnet (male)
In pairs or small flocks. Areas with scattered vegetation. (p195)

Black cap

Uniform grey back

White wing-bar

Blue-grey crown

Reddish-brown back

Two white wing-bars

Chaffinch (male)
Woodland, hedgerows, parks and gardens. Forms large flocks on cultivated land in winter. (p192)

Bullfinch
Stocky, bright but shy. Woodland edges and scrub. (p196)

> ➢ Similar species: Redpoll, Common Rosefinch, Red-breasted Flycatcher.

Redstart (male)
Mature oak
woodland. Quivers
its tail. (p165)

Grey back

Black throat

Orange tail

White
'eyebrow'

Blackish back

Whinchat (male)
Areas of long grass
with bushes, marshes.
(p166)

Uniform brown
upperparts

Robin
Often on the ground.
Can be very confiding
in parks and gardens.
(p163)

Face and breast
orange

Grey-green head

Yellow throat

Much black on head and back

Orange bar on
the shoulder

**Ortolan
Bunting (male)**
Not in Britain.
Scrub, dry hill-
sides, vineyards.
(p198)

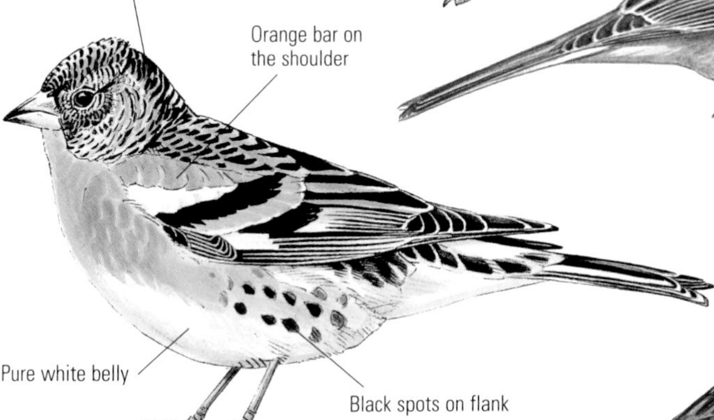

Grey head
striped black

Pure white belly

Black spots on flank

Brambling (male)
Winter visitor to Britain.
Often joins Chaffinch
flocks. (p192)

Grey breast

Rock Bunting
Not in Britain.
Mountains and
rocky hillsides on
the continent.
(p198)

Birds with red on the underparts (2)

A bird's size is always difficult to estimate. Try to compare it with a nearby bird that's familiar.

Slate-grey back

Red eye-ring

White moustache

Subalpine Warbler (male)
Not in Britain. Found in Mediterranean scrub. (p172)

Kingfisher
Always near water (rivers, lakes and also the coast in winter). Rapid flight just above the water. (p153)

Metallic blue back

Long dagger-shaped bill

Long curved bill

Large crest which can flare out

Black and white barred wings

Very short tail

Hoopoe
Unmistakeable. Rare visitor to Britain; common in southern Europe in hedgerows and gardens. (p154)

Great Spotted Woodpecker (male)

Climbs tree trunks and branches. Woodland, parks, gardens. (p155)

Whitish breast

Black-and-white back

Upperparts entirely slate-grey

Black eye-stripe

Nuthatch

Climbs up and down tree trunks and branches, often head-first. Often in tree tops. (p181)

Blue head

White patch on the back

Crossed mandibles

Red head and body

Dark brown wings

Crossbill

Conifer forests. Often occurs in flocks. (p195)

Range tail

Rock Thrush (male)

Not in Britain. Mountains and rocky coasts of southern Europe. (p168)

> Similar species:
> Middle Spotted Woodpecker, Red-throated Pipit.

Birds with red on the head

Try to pinpoint the red marking; is it on the forehead, crown, nape or cheek?

Black eye-stripe

Black back

Linnet (male)
In pairs in spring and summer, small flocks the rest of the year. Areas with scattered vegetation. (p195)

Grey head

Chestnut back

Red breast

Long tail

Large white wing-bar

Woodchat Shrike
Not in Britain. On the continent common in open woodland, olive groves. (p185)

White cheek

Buff back

Yellow patch on wing

Blackcap (female)
Occurs anywhere there are trees and bushes. Males have a black cap. (p174)

Underparts uniform pale grey

Goldfinch
Often perches on thistles to eat the seeds. (p194)

Powerful
pointed bill

Black crown

**Great Spotted
Woodpecker
(male)**
Climbs tree trunks
and branches.
(p155)

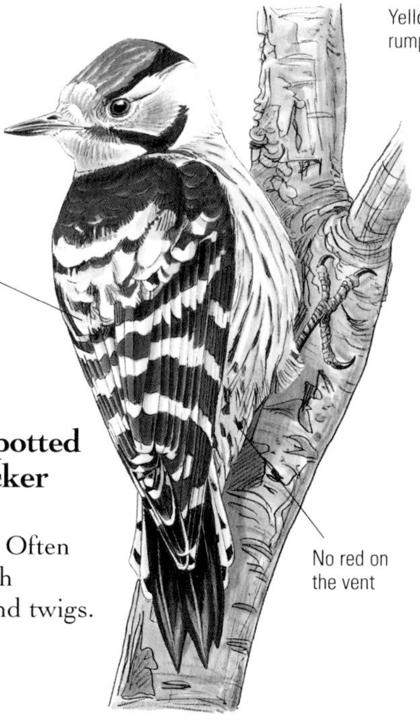

Large oval white
wing patch

Bright red vent

Black around eye

Upperparts
plain green

Yellow
rump

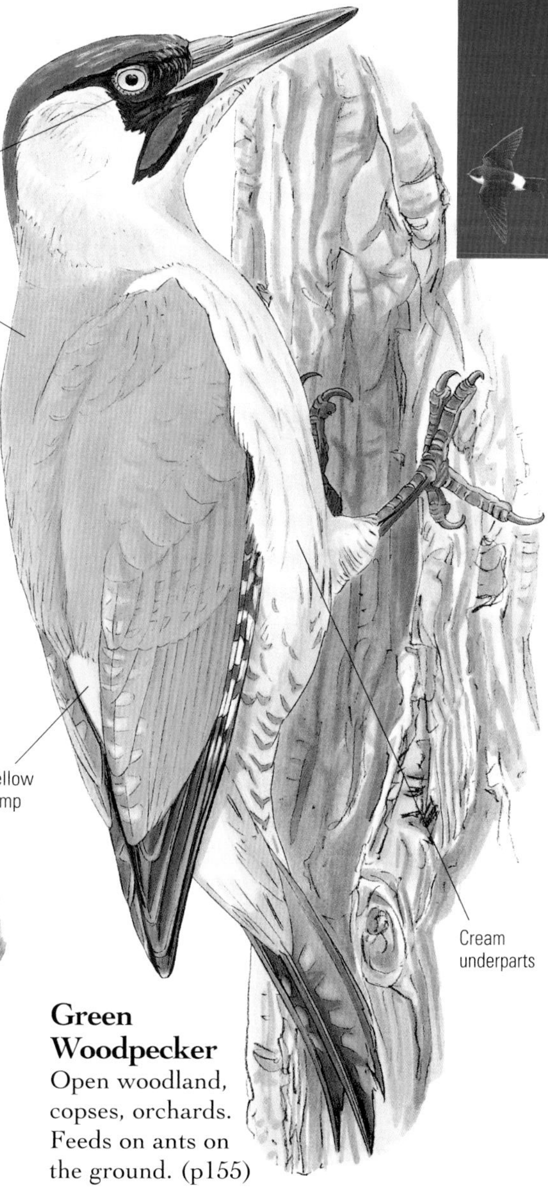

**Green
Woodpecker**
Open woodland,
copses, orchards.
Feeds on ants on
the ground. (p155)

Cream
underparts

Back black
barred with
white

**Lesser Spotted
Woodpecker
(male)**
Very small. Often
seen on high
branches and twigs.
(p156)

No red on
the vent

> See also: Chaffinch (page 92), Tree
Sparrow (page 26), Firecrest (page 48),
Swallow (page 46).
> Similar species: Common Rosefinch,
Redpoll, Middle Spotted Woodpecker,
Black Woodpecker.

White or colourful water birds (1)

Ducks and other water birds are usually easy to identify, as they often stay still and in view.

Mute Swan
(in threat posture)

Bottle-green head

Bright red bill
and knob

Shelduck
Mainly coastal. At a distance
appears black and white.
(p109)

Black knob on bill

Chestnut
breast-band

Very long neck

Orange bill

Mute Swan
Very visible and often
confiding. On all kinds
of inland water.
(p108)

All white plumage (grey-brown
in young birds)

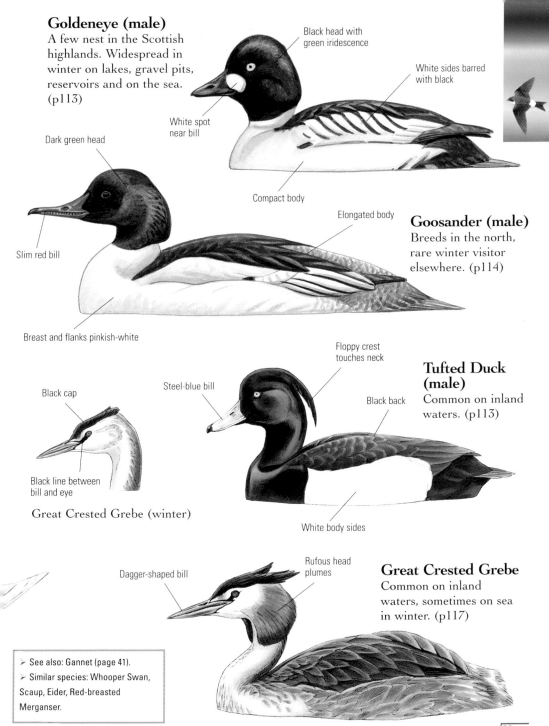

Goldeneye (male)

A few nest in the Scottish highlands. Widespread in winter on lakes, gravel pits, reservoirs and on the sea. (p113)

Black head with green iridescence

White sides barred with black

White spot near bill

Dark green head

Compact body

Slim red bill

Elongated body

Goosander (male)

Breeds in the north, rare winter visitor elsewhere. (p114)

Breast and flanks pinkish-white

Floppy crest touches neck

Tufted Duck (male)

Common on inland waters. (p113)

Black cap

Steel-blue bill

Black back

Black line between bill and eye

White body sides

Great Crested Grebe (winter)

Rufous head plumes

Dagger-shaped bill

Great Crested Grebe

Common on inland waters, sometimes on sea in winter. (p117)

> See also: Gannet (page 41).
> Similar species: Whooper Swan, Scaup, Eider, Red-breasted Merganser.

White or colourful water birds (2)

According to the light conditions, the same bird may appear completely dark or very colourful.

Brown head

White line extending behind the cheek

Slate-blue bill

Green mark surrounded with a yellow line

White horizontal line above black

Yellow triangular mark

Teal (male)
Anywhere there's water.
The smallest European duck.
(p110)

Long slender tail

Pintail (male)
Commonest in winter.
Estuaries, mudflats and
inland waters. (p111)

Bottle-green head

Large flat black bill

White breast

Shoveler (male)
A few breed in Britain. In winter on
inland waters and along the coast. (p111)

Rufous
flanks

Metallic green head

Mallard (male)
Europe's commonest duck, can be very confiding. (p110)

Yellow bill

Brown breast

Yellow forehead

Rufous head

Pinkish breast

Wigeon
A few breed in the north. Widespread in winter, often feeding on meadows. (p109)

Orange-brown head

Dark brown back

Red bill

Red-crested Pochard
Rare in Britain. Lakes and marshes in southern Europe. (p112)

White flanks

Reddish head

Grey and black bill

Grey back and flanks

Pochard (male)
Commoner in winter. Often with flocks of Tufted Duck. (p112)

Multicoloured birds

The few very colourful European birds are all distinctive and easy to identify.

Blue back

Long straight bill

Blue head

Rock Thrush (male)

Not in Britain. Mountains and, around the Mediterranean, on rocky escarpments and cliffs. (p168)

Orange underparts

Kingfisher

Always near water (rivers, lakes and the coast in winter). Direct, rapid flight low over water. (p153)

White patch on back

Very short tail

Long crest, often flattened backwards

Orange underparts

Orange tail

Long curved bill

Black and white barred back

Pinkish-buff underparts

Hoopoe

Very rare visitor to Britain, common in southern Europe. In flight recalls a large black and white butterfly. (p154)

Black and white barred wings

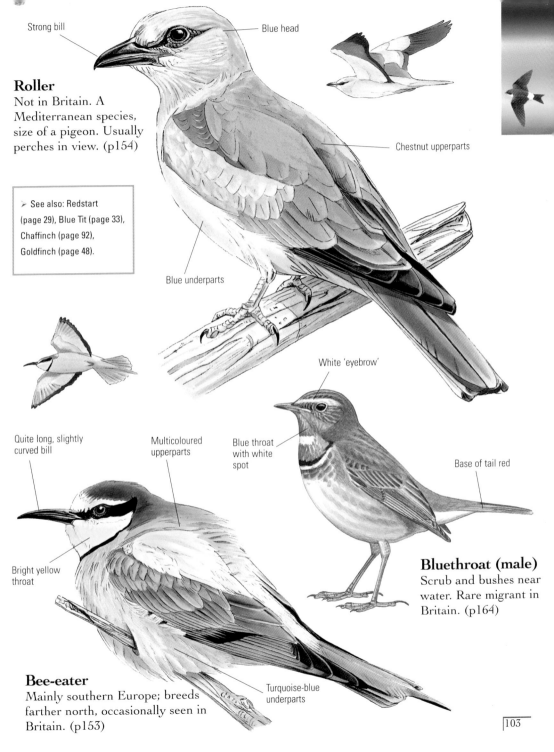

Strong bill

Blue head

Roller

Not in Britain. A Mediterranean species, size of a pigeon. Usually perches in view. (p154)

Chestnut upperparts

> See also: Redstart (page 29), Blue Tit (page 33), Chaffinch (page 92), Goldfinch (page 48).

Blue underparts

White 'eyebrow'

Quite long, slightly curved bill

Multicoloured upperparts

Blue throat with white spot

Base of tail red

Bright yellow throat

Bluethroat (male)

Scrub and bushes near water. Rare migrant in Britain. (p164)

Turquoise-blue underparts

Bee-eater

Mainly southern Europe; breeds farther north, occasionally seen in Britain. (p153)

Small distinctively coloured birds in flight

The way a bird flaps (continuous wing-beats or short bursts between glides) and flies (bounding up and down or in a straight line) can help identification.

Bullfinch (male)
(p196)

Black tail

Large white rump

Brambling (male)
(p192)

White rump

Two narrow white wing-bars

Two wide white wing-bars

Green rump

Chaffinch (male)
(p192)

Yellow patch near wing tip

Yellow sides to tail

Yellow sides to tail

Two yellow wing-bars

Yellow rump

Siskin (male)
(p194)

Wide yellow wing-bar

Upperparts striped black

Bright yellow rump

White rump

White markings on tail

Greenfinch (male) (p193)

Goldfinch
(p194)

Serin (male)
(p193)

Green upperparts

Bright yellow rump

Pointed tail

Green Woodpecker (male) (p155)

Blood-red wings

Grey upperparts

Bright yellow head and back

Black tail

Wallcreeper (female) (p182)

Golden Oriole (male) (p183)

Black wings

Pale grey back

Dark grey back

Black Redstart (male) (p165)

Orange tail

Orange tail

Redstart (male) (p165)

Whitish patch on wing

Species accounts

Mute Swan

Cygnus olor

This enormous white bird is difficult to miss, and graces many rivers, lakes and ornamental ponds with its presence. It is frequently very approachable. It occurs in most of the lowland areas of Britain and Ireland, and most birds are sedentary, although some move further south for winter and in very cold spells a few may arrive from the continent. In the breeding season pairs are highly territorial, fiercely driving off other water birds. The pair-bond is famously strong, with separation very unusual. Most cygnets are brownish-grey at first, the white adult plumage being acquired during the second year.

- **Length :** 1.45–1.6 m
- **Weight :** 7.6–14.3 kg
- **Food :** aquatic vegetation
- **Clutch :** 5–7 eggs (April–July)

Greylag Goose

Anser anser

The Greylag is the most widespread and the largest of the grey geese found in Britain, and the only one to breed here naturally, with a small population nesting in remote parts of Scotland. However, over the last 50 years many feral populations have also become established, and it now breeds throughout Britain on many of the larger waters. Numbers in winter increase markedly as the total Icelandic population comes to Britain for the winter; most birds staying in Scotland or Ireland. These migrants tend to use traditional sites and it can be a marvellous experience to watch hundreds of birds together, often in the company of other species, on protected sites in the north and west of the country.

- **Length :** 75–90 cm
- **Weight :** 2.1–4.6 kg
- **Food :** grasses, tubers, seeds and grain
- **Clutch :** 4–6 eggs (April–May)

Shelduck
Tadorna tadorna

- **Length :** 58–67 cm
- **Weight :** 560 g–1.5 kg
- **Food :** molluscs, crustaceans and algae
- **Clutch :** 8–15 eggs (April–July)

This large duck is essentially a coastal species. It breeds and spends the winter on much of our coastline, especially where there are muddy estuaries, such as the Forth, Wash, Humber and Morecambe Bay. A large proportion of Europe's breeding population migrates to the Wadden Sea in Germany in the late summer to moult, leaving their part-grown ducklings in 'crèches' in the care of one or two adults. With an increasing population more birds are now recorded inland, a few pairs breeding far from the coast. Nevertheless, Shelduck are most frequently encountered on coastal mudflats, often in small groups. They breed in burrows, often using abandoned rabbit-holes.

Wigeon
Anas penelope

- **Length :** 45–50 cm
- **Weight :** 530 g–1.1 kg
- **Food :** vegetation in the water and on land
- **Clutch :** 6–10 eggs (May–June)

This beautiful medium-sized duck often gives its presence away by the male's far-carrying, whistling *whee-oo* call. Females are rich chocolate-brown, and, as with other ducks, males assume a drab 'eclipse' plumage during the late summer moult. A few breed in Britain each year, mainly in northern England and central and northern Scotland, but it is much more numerous and widespread in winter. Most wintering birds frequent coastal sites, favouring areas with undisturbed expanses of water and suitable short grass nearby for feeding.

Teal
Anas crecca

This is the smallest European duck and one of the most common and widespread in Britain and Ireland as well as on the continent. It is an active and agile duck; watching small flocks springing from the water's surface with their fast zigzag flight, whilst giving their soft whistling calls, is a marvellous experience. It is quite widespread as a breeding species, occupying many small marshes and lochs in Scotland and Ireland, but is much rarer as a breeding bird further south. In winter this is reversed with the species being more numerous in the south. It occurs almost anywhere that there are waters rich with vegetation, both inland and on the coast. Females are mottled brown, with plain faces and a green wing flash.

- **Length :** 34–38 cm
- **Weight :** 185–450 g
- **Food :** seeds of aquatic plants, some invertebrates
- **Clutch :** 8–12 eggs (April–June)

Mallard
Anas platyrhynchos

The Mallard is not only the best-known and commonest British duck, but is also one of the most widespread of British and European birds. There's hardly an area of fresh water where it doesn't occur and many birds are found along the coast, particularly on saltmarshes during the winter. It is the female (photo) that gives the well-known *quack*, males make a softer, more nasal call. The male is the only duck to have curly tail-feathers. The Mallard is the ancestor of the domestic duck, and strange ducks with white, black or variegated plumage are often the result of hybrids between wild Mallards and their domestic cousins.

- **Length :** 50–65 cm
- **Weight :** 750 g–1.57 kg
- **Food :** plants seeds and aquatic insects
- **Clutch :** 9–13 eggs (March–July)

Pintail
Anas acuta

- **Length :** 51–66 cm
- **Weight :** 550 g–1.3 kg
- **Food :** plants, seeds and invertebrates
- **Clutch :** 7–9 eggs (April–June)

This elegant duck is very rare as a breeding species in Britain; a few nest most years near the Thames estuary, the Humber and Ouse Washes area and scattered localities in Scotland. In winter it is much more widespread with most birds found on the larger estuaries; and although many inland waters have a few birds only the Nene and Ouse Washes hold important numbers. Although the male is easily recognised, the brown female (see photo) is very similar to other female dabbling ducks; its elongated shape and bluish bill help distinguish it.

Shoveler
Anas clypeata

- **Length :** 45–50 cm
- **Weight :** 470 g–1 kg
- **Food :** invertebrates and aquatic plants
- **Clutch :** 9–11 eggs (May–June)

The male Shoveler is a very distinctive bird with a bright white breast and chestnut flanks. Females are much duller and can easily be mistaken for female Mallards; look for the distinctive large bill and, in flight, the pale grey forewing. This is an uncommon breeding species in Britain, occurring on invertebrate-rich shallow waters, mainly in the south-east of the country. It is more numerous in winter with many birds arriving in Britain from farther north in November where, as in summer, numbers are highest in the southern half of the country.

Red-crested Pochard
Netta rufina

The male is a very handsome duck, hard to confuse with any other species except perhaps the Common Pochard at a distance. As in most ducks the female (photo) is less colourful. It is rare in Britain and the small numbers that breed and winter on reed-fringed ponds and lakes in the southeast are thought to be of captive origin although it is possible that a few wild birds from the continent occur each year too. The species is common in parts of southern Europe; it is increasingly easy to see throughout the year in inland wetlands in southern France and particularly in winter in the Camargue. It often associates with flocks of other freshwater diving ducks, such as Common Pochard and Tufted Duck.

- **Length :** 53–57 cm
- **Weight :** 850 g–1.4 kg
- **Food :** aquatic plants and seeds, some invertebrates
- **Clutch :** 8–10 eggs (May–June)

Pochard
Aythya ferina

The handsome Pochard is one of our commoner ducks. Only a few pairs breed in Britain, but they are scattered throughout the country with the highest numbers in the south; it seems to be on the decrease in Scotland. In late summer birds flock together to moult; favourite sites are Abberton Reservoir in Essex and the well-known Rutland Water. Many birds arrive from northern Europe in the winter and then the species becomes common on nearly all large freshwater lakes, reservoirs, gravel pits and even city park boating lakes. It is widespread on the continent. Females are warm brown, with vague pale face markings and dark eyes.

- **Length :** 42–49 cm
- **Weight :** 470 g–1.3 kg
- **Food :** aquatic plants and their seeds, some invertebrates
- **Clutch :** 8–10 eggs (April–June)

Tufted Duck
Aythya fuligula

- **Length** : 40–47 cm
- **Weight** : 400–950 g
- **Food** : molluscs, also insects, and seeds of aquatic plants
- **Clutch** : 8–11 eggs (May–July)

This is one of the most readily identifiable of our ducks; but females lack the characteristic striking black and white plumage and drooping crest, as do males during the 'eclipse' moult in late summer – look for the yellow eyes, and a dull brown shadow of the summer male's pattern. The first known breeding record in Britain occurred in Yorkshire in 1849 and since then the species has spread and increased to such an extent that it is now common on many inland waters, even town park lakes. It is easy to see on any relatively large inland water during the winter. As with the Pochard, it has prospered with the creation of a large number of gravel pits since the 1960s.

Goldeneye
Bucephala clangula

- **Length** : 42–50 cm
- **Weight** : 500 g–1.25 kg
- **Food** : molluscs, crustaceans and, aquatic insects
- **Clutch** : 8–11 eggs (May–June)

This species is uncommon in Britain as it is at the southern edge of its range here. However, it has regularly bred in the Highlands of Scotland, since 1970 and the small numbers that continue to nest often use nest boxes provided for them – the species' natural nest-site is a hole in a tree. It is much more widespread and numerous in winter both on inland waters and around the coast, although it becomes increasingly less frequent towards the south. Goldeneyes can stay underwater for a long time, so patience is required to find them in the middle of a large expanse of water on a cold, windy winter's day. Females (photo) are grey with brown heads but have the distinctive yellow eye.

Goosander

Mergus merganser

This is one of the so-called 'sawbill' ducks, named for their long slender bills with serrations that help them grip the fish they catch. The Goosander is the most widespread of the group in Britain. As a breeding bird it is found mainly along tree-lined or boulder-strewn rivers in the north of England and in Scotland, where it nests in holes in trees or among boulders. In winter it is much more widespread but never common; look for it on large expanses of inland water or off the coast, particularly in estuaries. Northern birds come to spend winter in Britain, they are more easily found during spells of hard weather. Females (photo) are grey and white with brown heads.

- **Length :** 58–66 cm
- **Weight :** 900 g–2.16 kg
- **Food :** small fish, a few molluscs and crustaceans
- **Clutch :** 8–11 eggs (May–July)

Red-legged Partridge

Alectoris rufa

The handsome Red-legged Partridge was first introduced into Britain from the continent around 200 years ago, as a gamebird. It is now quite a familiar bird of open agricultural land, especially in the south-eastern half of the country. It can be found year-round, mainly on flat, dry, open ground when it is usually seen in pairs or family groups. It occurs naturally in the south of Europe where it is most commonly found in dry sunny areas. It is usually seen on the ground but will readily take off and disappear with a fast low flight if it is disturbed or threatened.

- **Length :** 32–38 cm
- **Weight :** 340–630 g
- **Food :** seeds, leaves and insects
- **Clutch :** 10–16 eggs (May–June)

Grey Partridge
Perdix perdix

- **Length** : 29–31 cm
- **Weight** : 310–450 g
- **Food** : seeds, leaves and berries
- **Clutch** : 10–20 eggs (May–June)

Our native partridge is much more widespread than its larger cousin the Red-legged Partridge. It has declined a great deal over the last few decades but can still be found over much of Britain where crops are grown and where it can find enough hedgerows and other cover to provide safe nest sites. It is absent from high altitudes and much of the very north and west of the country, and is quite a rare species in Ireland. It usually runs away from danger rather than flying. If you are looking for the species, you're much more likely to be successful if you watch from a slow-moving car rather than on foot.

Quail
Coturnix coturnix

- **Length** : 16–19 cm
- **Weight** : 70–150 g
- **Food** : small seeds, insects, spiders, earthworms
- **Clutch** : 8–13 eggs (May–June)

Our smallest gamebird and the only one which migrates, the enigmatic Quail is no bigger than a thrush. Very secretive, it spends the late spring and summer hidden in long grass and crops, making it very difficult to see; but the male gives its presence away with its characteristic, easily identified and often repeated *wet-my-lips* song. Every so often there is a so-called 'Quail year' in which more birds than normal arrive to breed; there's more chance of finding a bird in such a year and the grasslands of Wiltshire and Dorset are the most likely areas. Though quite rare in Britain, it is commoner in southern Europe.

Pheasant

Phasianus colchicus

Common throughout most of Europe, the well-known Pheasant is an introduced species to Britain, brought here many centuries ago by the Normans or Romans. The male (photo) is a distinctive large ground-dwelling bird, females and young are drab. Young pheasants (like most young game birds) can fly when still quite small at which time they can be confused with other species, especially as they lack long tails. Easy to see on flat agricultural land in the south and east, especially in wet areas, the species is rarer or absent from much of far west and north. It does not occur at high altitudes or in very dense woodland.

- **Length :** 53–89 cm
- **Weight :** 1.1–1.6 kg
- **Food :** seeds and also some insects
- **Clutch :** 8–15 eggs (March–June)

Little Grebe

Tachybaptus ruficollis

A tiny species, this is the smallest swimming bird in Europe. It mainly occurs on freshwater, lakes, ponds and slow-flowing rivers, wherever there is ample aquatic vegetation. As with other grebes it dives to hunt and can stay underwater for what seems a long time. It may reappear quite a distance from when it first dived, even surfacing amongst vegetation; so it's not always easy to locate. Relatively common in most of lowland Britain, it can be found wherever there's suitable stretches of water, but doesn't occur at high altitudes. It may disappear from northern areas after severe winters. It moults its reddish and black colours in winter, becoming much paler and duller – look out for the truncated, 'powder-puff' rear.

- **Length :** 25–29 cm
- **Weight :** 120–320 g
- **Food :** aquatic insects, small fishes
- **Clutch :** 4–6 eggs (April–July)

Great Crested Grebe

Podiceps cristatus

- **Length :** 46–51 cm
- **Weight :** 650 g–1.4 kg
- **Food :** exclusively small fish
- **Clutch :** 2–6 eggs (April–July)

This handsome species has colourful head plumes in spring and summer, which are used during the elaborate courtship dances performed by pairs before nesting. For the first few days after hatching the humbug-striped chicks will often be carried on the back of one or other of the parents. The species was nearly wiped out in Britain during the middle of the 19th century, as birds were hunted for their head feathers for the millinery trade – protests against this trade led to the birth of the Royal Society for the Protection of Birds. Today the Great Crested Grebe can be seen on many inland waters in England, Wales and Ireland, though is less widespread in Scotland. Quite a few birds can be seen on the sea in winter.

Black-necked Grebe

Podiceps nigricollis

- **Length :** 28–34 cm
- **Weight :** 230–450 g
- **Food :** aquatic insects and their larvae
- **Clutch :** 3–4 eggs (April–June)

A beautiful, active little grebe, this species is quite difficult to see in Britain. The first confirmed breeding attempt in Britain was in 1904 and very gradually the species has increased. A few now breed each year on vegetation-rich inland waters scattered throughout the country, their whereabouts often kept secret so as to avoid disturbance. It tends to use estuaries more in winter, the best places to look are around Anglesey and the Solent; the best period September and October. Even on the continent it's not an easy species to find; a late spring visit to the Brenne in central France is probably the best option. In winter the orange cheek tufts disappear and the plumage becomes black and white (photo).

Gannet
Morus bassanus

The Gannet is a true seabird, breeding in large colonies on remote sea-cliffs around the Atlantic and feeding on fish caught at sea. Nearly three-quarters of the world population breeds in Britain and numbers are increasing, which should make it an easy species to see; but most nest on remote islands; the most accessible colonies are those at Bempton cliffs in Humberside and at Bass Rock near Edinburgh. They are present at breeding sites throughout the year, with maximum numbers any time between April and September. Gannets are also readily visible from ferries crossing the channel between England and France, if the weather's favourable it's often possible to see many birds at close quarters during a single crossing.

- **Length :** 87 cm–1 m
- **Weight :** 2.3–3.6 kg
- **Food :** exclusively sea fish
- **Clutch :** 1 egg (April–June)

Cormorant
Phalacrocorax carbo

A large, mainly dark water bird that is increasingly easy to see in Britain. As a breeding species it was once confined to our coasts, with a preference for nesting on cliffs and rocky islets along the west coast. During the 1980s it started breeding inland, in trees, and today one of the largest colonies anywhere is at Abberton Reservoir. The origin of the inland-nesting birds is not known but most appear to be of the same race that breeds on our coasts, although a few 'continental' birds (many of which have white on the head as in the illustration above) are also present. In winter it is more widespread, present along much of the coast and in small numbers at most large inland waters.

- **Length :** 80 cm–1 m
- **Weight :** 1.7–3.2 kg
- **Food :** aquatic and freshwater fish
- **Clutch :** 3–4 eggs (April–June)

Shag
Phalacrocorax aristotelis

A smaller version of the Cormorant, the Shag is almost exclusively marine, although the occasional bird is found inland after a storm. Most nest in colonies on remote islands and extensive sea cliffs, but smaller colonies can be found along much of the west and north coastline of Britain; anywhere clockwise between the Isle of Wight and Bempton Cliffs in Humberside. It is very rare on the east and south coasts between these two points. Quite sedentary, it never ventures far out to sea and can be seen at any favourite site throughout the year.

- **Length** : 65–80 cm
- **Weight** : 1.8–2.2 kg
- **Food** : aquatic fish and crustaceans
- **Clutch** : 3 eggs (March–June)

Night Heron
Nycticorax nycticorax

A very rare visitor to Britain, this small, stocky, migrant heron is quite a common breeding species in some of the areas of larger wetlands in southern Europe. There is a free-flying colony at Edinburgh Zoo, which provides the chance to become acquainted with the species. It isn't always easy to find, being mainly active when there's little light and spending the daytime hidden in waterside trees. On the continent it is often quite common and is increasing; it can be seen between April and October in suitable habitat in southern Europe, such as the Camargue and Ebro Delta, when its distinctive *kwak* call often gives it away.

- **Length** : 58–65 cm
- **Weight** : 530–800 g
- **Food** : amphibians, small fish, insects
- **Clutch** : 3–4 eggs (May–June)

Cattle Egret

Bubulcus ibis

The lively and very widespread Cattle Egret nearly always feeds in flocks in association with large mammals, whether elephants and antelopes in parts of Africa, or with domestic live-stock in much of the temperate part of the world, often in marshy or wet areas. As these animals graze they disturb insects, which the egrets catch. It has bred in south-west Spain for a long time, started breeding in France in the 1960s and may well spread to Britain in the foreseeable future. At the moment it is still quite a rare visitor here, so to be sure of seeing breeding birds a visit to the wet-lands of southern Europe is necessary.

- **Length :** 48–53 cm
- **Weight :** 300–400 g
- **Food :** large terrestrial insects
- **Clutch :** 4–5 eggs (May–July)

Little Egret

Egretta garzetta

Once a rare species here, a marked northward expansion of range in Europe over the past fifty years or so resulted in the first ever breeding of the species in Britain in 1997. Since then num-bers have increased rapidly and it is now a rela-tively common sight in many estuaries along the south and south-east coasts. A large, bright white bird feeding in an open habitat is usually quite easy to find; the largest breeding concentrations of the species are presently at Foulness in Essex and Northward Hill in Kent but it is increasing and may occur at any suitable shallow water in the southern half of Britain.

- **Length :** 55–65 cm
- **Weight :** 350–460 g
- **Food :** fish, amphibians and insects
- **Clutch :** 3–5 eggs (May–July)

Great Egret
Ardea alba

Another species of heron on the increase, the Great Egret was very rare in western Europe until the 1970s. Since then, numbers have gradually increased and today it is numerous at some western European wetlands in winter. It is still, however, very rare in western Europe as a breeding species. In Britain it remains a rare visitor, although sightings are increasing. There are no regularly reliable sites in Britain, so a visit to the continent is the only way to be sure of seeing this impressive species; it is most abundant in western Europe during the winter, September to March, at any major wetland.

- **Length :** 85 cm–1.02 m
- **Weight :** 900 g–1.7 kg
- **Food :** fish, insects and other small animals
- **Clutch :** 3–5 eggs (April–June)

Grey Heron
Ardea cinerea

This familiar species is by far the most widespread and easily observed of the heron family in Britain. It is present year-round and is common almost anywhere that sufficient fish can be found, along lake and reservoir edges, including town park lakes, rivers and shallow parts of the coast, although it is much less numerous at higher altitudes. It usually nests in large colonies in the tops of large trees but will nest lower down where protection is adequate. Its breeding season is long (February to July) and during this time the same nest may be used by two different pairs.

- **Length :** 90–98 cm
- **Weight :** 1.2–1.9 kg
- **Food :** fish, amphibians and rodents
- **Clutch :** 3–5 eggs (February–July)

Purple Heron
Ardea purpurea

This handsome heron is a migrant that winters in sub-saharan Africa and breeds in the southern wetlands of western Europe. It is a very rare visitor to Britain; Minsmere on the Suffolk coast a good track record for attracting the species, but even there it is extremely infrequent. It can be relatively common at some of the major wetlands with extensive reedbeds in the south of Europe between late April and September; the nearest good sites to Britain are Sologne, Brenne, the Dombes and Camargue. It feeds in much more seccluded spots than its larger cousin, the Grey Heron, can be much more secretive and thus may take some finding.

- **Length :** 78–90 cm
- **Weight :** 530 g–1.2 kg
- **Food :** small fish, amphibians and insects
- **Clutch :** 4–5 eggs (May–June)

Black Stork
Ciconia nigra

A very distinctive species, the Black Stork is easy to identify but not at all easy to find. It migrates between wintering grounds in southern Africa to breed in some of the more extensively forested areas of Europe, such as the uplands of Extremadura in Spain. For such a large and strikingly patterned bird, it can be very difficult to find and watch as it is shy and secretive. It is an extremely rare visitor to Britain, so to be sure of seeing this species a trip abroad is necessary and even then success is difficult to guarantee.

- **Length :** 95–100 cm
- **Weight :** 2.4–3.0 kg
- **Food :** especially small fish
- **Clutch :** 3–5 eggs (April–June)

White Stork
Ciconia ciconia

O f very rare occurrence in Britain, on the continent the White Stork often builds its large nest near to areas of human habitation and not infrequently on the roofs of buildings, often picking the highest vantage-point in a village, such as the church tower. It is one of the earliest migrants to return to its breeding grounds in Europe, with many birds back before the end of February. The species is quite common in many parts of Spain between March and September and its numbers are increasing in France, especially along the Atlantic coast. It now nests quite close to Britain with a small but growing population on the Normandy coast (near Marquenterre and the Cotentin marshes).

- **Length :** 1–1.15 m
- **Weight :** 2.3–4.4 kg
- **Food :** insects and other small creatures
- **Clutch :** 3–5 eggs (March–April)

Spoonbill
Platalea leucorodia

T his striking bird is a rare but regularly occurring species in Britain, With increasing numbers breeding on the Atlantic seaboard on the other side of the Channel and North Sea it is not surprising that it has become more regular here and has attempted to nest on several occasions, mainly on the east coast. It favours estuaries and lagoons along the coast but can occur wherever there are extensive areas of invertebrate-rich shallow waters. East-coast wetlands like Minsmere on the Suffolk coast are good places to look. The nearest regular breeding site on the continent is at Marquenterre, on the Baie de Somme, in Normandy.

- **Length :** 80–90 cm
- **Weight :** 1.7–2.0 kg
- **Food :** aquatic insects, small fish, crustceans
- **Clutch :** 3–5 eggs (April–July)

Greater Flamingo

Phoenicopterus ruber

Flamingos seen at large in Britain are likely to be escapees from zoos or wildlife parks. In Europe this is very much a Mediterranean species. It can be seen throughout the year on most salt-pans and lagoons along the Spanish and French Mediterranean coast, although birds tend to concentrate around a smaller number of favoured nesting areas in spring and summer. Where it does occur it can occur in very large numbers; the well known nesting site at the Fangassier in the south-east corner of the Camargue attracts thousands of birds ever year. A trip to the Camargue to see the spectacle of lines of bright pink flamingos flying in all directions can provide for a very memorable experience.

- **Length :** 1.4–1.65 m
- **Weight :** 2.1–4.1 kg
- **Food :** small aquatic creatures, especially brine shrimps
- **Clutch :** 1 egg (April–June)

Honey Buzzard

Pernis apivorus

The Honey Buzzard is longer-winged and smaller-headed than the much more numerous Buzzard, but good views are necessary to be sure of its identity. This mainly insectivorous bird is a summer migrant, returning from Africa in May, and most have left Europe by mid-September. Although it may breed in any well-wooded countryside it is very rare in Britain and sites are kept secret to keep human disturbance to a minimum. It is much easier to find in much of continental Europe and is a relatively common breeding species in much of the countryside of central and north-east France. However, it is a shy bird whilst breeding, so patience is often necessary to see it well.

- **Length :** 52–60 cm
- **Weight :** 620–960 g
- **Food :** wasps, bumblebees and their larvae
- **Clutch :** 1–3 eggs (June–July)

Black Kite
Milvus migrans

- **Length :** 47–55 cm
- **Weight :** 630–940 g
- **Food :** dead animals, rodents, insects
- **Clutch :** 2–3 eggs (April–June)

Another migrant bird of prey, the Black Kite is present at its European breeding grounds between late February and late August. Although a very rare visitor to Britain, it is quite common in parts of nearby Europe, becoming more numerous further south. Most birds breed in the vicinity of water, in areas with large lakes or reservoirs or near large sluggish rivers. Much of its food is scavenged; it can often be seen taking dead fish from the water surface, flying low over countryside roads looking for traffic victims or in meadows when hay-making is in progress when it readily takes large insects. It often forages in flocks.

Red Kite
Milvus milvus

- **Length :** 58–64 cm
- **Weight :** 780g–1.25 kg
- **Food :** dead animals, rodents
- **Clutch :** 2–3 eggs (April–June)

Britain's populalation of this magnificent resident bird of prey was once reduced to a handful of breeding pairs in a remote area of central Wales. However, thanks to avid protection there and recent reintroduction programs in England and Scotland the species has increased so much that it's now a common and frequent sight in many areas of Britain. The best places to see the species are still near the seven release sites, especially the Chilterns on the Oxfordshire/Buckinghamshire border, and in its original stronghold in central Wales. However, they are spreading fast, and much of Britain's countryside could be home to Red Kites in the near future. Red Kites are easy to see as they soar and circle in search of carrion to scavenge.

Egyptian Vulture

Neophron percnopterus

It is extremely unlikely that this small vulture will be seen in Britain. It's a rare summer migrant to some areas of southern Europe, and even there numbers are quite low. It arrives in late March and leaves in September, nesting on inland cliffs overlooking valleys or deep gorges, sometimes on the edge of a colony of Griffon Vultures and other birds of prey. Very few now breed in France (the Alpilles hills north of the Camargue and Argelès-Gazost or Laruns in the Pyrenees are reliable sites) or Italy, but it is slightly commoner in Greece and Turkey, and is still relatively common in parts of Spain and Portugal.

- **Length :** 55–65 cm
- **Weight :** 1.6–2.4 kg
- **Food :** dead animals (including their skins)
- **Clutch :** 2 eggs (April–May)

Griffon Vulture

Gyps fulvus

This enormous bird of prey does not occur in Britain. It nests in colonies on cliffs, and although still very locally distributed in western Europe, its numbers have recently increased considerably, probably as a result of more enlightened attitudes towards its scavenging habits. The nearest colony to Britain, in the Grands Causses area of the Cevennes in southern France, is the result of a recent successful reintroduction program. Elsewhere it can be seen in good numbers in many parts of the Pyrenees (near Gavarnie and at a large colony near Laruns) and in many areas in Spain.

- **Length :** 95 cm–1.05 m
- **Weight :** 6.2–8.5 kg
- **Food :** dead animals (especially domestic livestock)
- **Clutch :** 1 egg (February–May)

Short-toed Eagle

Circaetus gallicus

A summer visitor to southern Europe that feeds mainly on reptiles, it is not surprising that this large species has very seldom been seen in Britain. This eagle is an impressive bird that is relatively easy to identify, its slow hovering flight whilst searching for potential prey, often at quite a height, is distinctive. The Short-toed Eagle is relatively common in much of the southern half of France and throughout Spain, Portugal, Italy and Mediterranean countries further east, wherever there is open unspoilt countryside with plenty of snakes and lizards. It is generally easiest to find in hilly or mountainous areas such as the Cevennes, Alps or Pyrenees.

- **Length :** 62–67 cm
- **Weight :** 1.2–2.3 kg
- **Food :** snakes and lizards
- **Clutch :** 1 egg (April–July)

Marsh Harrier

Circus aeruginosus

In Britain the Marsh Harrier was reduced to just one pair in 1971 (breeding at Minsmere in Suffolk), its decline due to persecution and the effects of chemical pollutants in the environment. Since the ban on these products the population has recovered remarkably, and there are now some 300 pairs breeding in the country, most still in eastern England (particularly East Anglia) but with isolated groups and pairs spread throughout many areas as far as the Orkneys. Present in Britain year-round, Marsh Harriers are easy to see in the right habitat as they glide low over reedbeds, wings held in a shallow V-shape. Females (photo) are often very dark, males have a more variegated grey, sandy and black pattern.

- **Length :** 48–56 cm
- **Weight :** 400 g–1.1 kg
- **Food :** small rodents and birds
- **Clutch :** 3–6 eggs (April–June)

Hen Harrier

Circus cyaneus

Most Hen Harriers that breed in Britain do so on heather moorland in the north and west. This brings them into conflict with grouse-shooting interests and it seems likely that their gradual increase in numbers would be more rapid without illegal persecution. Although resident they tend to move away from their breeding grounds for the winter, most birds moving to the coast or near the larger rivers. Winter is often an easier time to see the species but numbers are not high and an encounter with this charismatic bird, whether a ghostly grey male or brown, white-rumped female, is often a chance affair. It is widespread but often local on the continent, commonest in France and Scandinavia.

- **Length :** 44–52 cm
- **Weight :** 300–710 g
- **Food :** small birds, rodents
- **Clutch :** 4–6 eggs (May–July)

Montagu's Harrier

Circus pygargus

Unlike the similar Hen Harrier, the Montagu's Harrier is a summer migrant, returning from Africa during April and departing in September. It is the smallest and rarest of the British harriers; although numbers fluctuate there are no long-term indications of an increase or decline. It tends to nest in crops in the south-east of the country, although pairs have bred further north and west and at one time the West Country was a favoured area. It is more widespread and commoner in many parts of the continent and a quite common sight in summer over open agricultural land in much of southern Europe. As with Hen Harriers, males are grey and females brown.

- **Length :** 42–47 cm
- **Weight :** 230–445 g
- **Food :** small birds, rodents
- **Clutch :** 4–5 eggs (May–July)

Sparrowhawk
Accipiter nisus

- **Length** : 28–38 cm
- **Weight** : 110–340 g
- **Food** : small birds only
- **Clutch** : 4–6 eggs (April–June)

The Sparrowhawk was one of the species that suffered most from the extensive use of organochloride pesticides by the farming community in the 1950s and 1960s. The population has recovered to such an extent that today it is, with the Kestrel, the commonest and most widespread bird of prey over much of Europe including Britain, found in all well-wooded areas. However, unlike the Kestrel it is not always easy to see well, usually staying hidden as it hunts small birds with a low, rapid, agile flight. Sparrowhawks regularly take small birds from garden bird tables, and may drop onto the lawn to pluck their victim. Females (photo) are much larger than males, which have reddish underparts.

Buzzard
Buteo buteo

- **Length** : 51–57 cm
- **Weight** : 450 g–1.35 kg
- **Food** : small mammals such as voles and rabbits
- **Clutch** : 2–4 eggs (April–June)

This is Britain's commonest large raptor; thanks to better protection, less persecution and the ban on the most harmful pesticides Buzzards can now be seen over much of the British Isles. Although it is most numerous and easiest to see in the remoter parts of the west and north, it may be found anywhere in the countryside with extensive areas of meadows, heath or moorland with hedgerows, copses and woodland. It is most easily found during fine days in early spring when pairs glide together high above their territories giving their mewing call. It is common on the continent where the French name *Buse variable* is appropriate, as plumage colour varies from one bird to another.

Golden Eagle

Aquila chrysaetos

The magnificent Golden Eagle is a rare bird in Britain, breeding only in some of the wilder and remoter parts of Scotland, particularly the Highlands and Western Isles; one pair has bred in the Lake District. Adults (photo) rarely leave their breeding grounds but immature birds (illustration) may range over a wider area. The nest is usually built on an inaccessible cliff, birds often use the same site from one year to the next, adding to the nest each year – it can become an enormous structure. Seeing a Golden Eagle can be a chance affair but once in breeding territory keep watching the sky, one may eventually appear along a ridge, gliding on long straight wings.

- **Length** : 75–88 cm
- **Weight** : 2.8–6.6 kg
- **Food** : mammals (rabbits, hares), carrion and birds
- **Clutch** : 2 eggs (March–May)

Booted Eagle

Hieraaetus pennatus

A small, Buzzard-sized, migrant eagle, this species confusingly occurs in two colour phases. Almost never seen in Britain, even on the continent it is never common so that seeing the species is not easy. It occupies much of southern Europe – Spain and Portugal have most birds while central and north-eastern France are the closest areas to Britain where it nests. It arrives in March and leaves in October; during this time a visit to the foothills of the Pyrenees provides a good chance of finding it. Take a good look at all medium-sized raptors. Pale-phase birds resemble pale Buzzards, while dark-phase birds, which are more numerous, can easily be confused with Black Kites.

- **Length** : 45–53 cm
- **Weight** : 500 g–1.25 kg
- **Food** : birds, lizards and rodents
- **Clutch** : 2 eggs (May–June)

Osprey
Pandion haliaetus

The fish-eating Osprey was exterminated from Britain 100 years ago, with the last few pairs nesting into the early 20th century. It returned naturally in the 1950s when a single pair nested at the famous Loch Garten site in the Highlands. Since then, despite vandalism and egg-collecting the population has gradually grown to reach at least 200 pairs, mostly in Scotland with a few in England and Wales. During their migration between Europe and West Africa in April and September they may turn up at almost any large inland water, or along the coast. Breeding birds can be seen at Rutland Water and many sites in the Highlands. It is rare but increasing elsewhere in Europe.

- **Length :** 50–58 cm
- **Weight :** 1.1–2 kg
- **Food :** fish only, caught by surface grabs
- **Clutch :** 2–3 eggs (April–June)

Kestrel
Falco tinnunculus

The dainty Kestrel is one of Britain and Europe's most common and widespread birds of prey. It is regularly seen hovering low over grassland and motorway verges as it searches for rodents. A resident species throughout much of Britain, it breeds in nearly all areas except Shetland; some birds leave higher ground and northern areas to winter further south and east when birds from the continent also increase the population. It can be seen in many types of habitat, even in town centres, but shows a strong preference for agricultural land where its favoured prey, voles, are most numerous. Females are chestnut-brown, males have grey heads and tails.

- **Length :** 32–35 cm
- **Weight :** 135–315 g
- **Food :** rodents, birds, insects
- **Clutch :** 3–6 eggs (April–June)

Hobby
Falco subbuteo

Another migrant bird of prey, the dashing Hobby arrives in Europe during April and May, and returns to Africa during September and October. It is not common but has increased recently and can now be found in many open areas with scattered trees in southern England, the Midlands, East Anglia and the south of Yorkshire. It hunts insects, especially dragonflies, and small birds, chasing even Swifts and Swallows in its fast hunting flight. In summer when it is feeding chicks it tends to take more birds, and the fledglings practice their skills on immature and inexperienced young birds. It is widely distributed over much of the continent but never numerous.

- **Length :** 30–36 cm
- **Weight :** 130–340 g
- **Food :** small birds, insects
- **Clutch :** 3 eggs (June–July)

Peregrine
Falco peregrinus

The Peregrine epitomises speed and power and inspires thoughts of wild places. It declined alarmingly as a result of the widespread use of organochloride pesticides in the 1950s and 60s, but has now increased again to numbers that were never seen in historic times. Most birds breed on cliffs and crags in the west and north of the country, where they feed on largish birds such as pigeons, caught in flight. However, more and more birds occupying areas further south and east, and some have even started breeding in large cities where tall buildings replace traditional cliff nest-sites and where there are ample street pigeons to catch. It is uncommon yet widespread in rugged areas on the continent.

- **Length :** 36–48 cm
- **Weight :** 580 g–1.2 kg
- **Food :** birds only
- **Clutch :** 3–4 eggs (March–April)

Moorhen
Gallinula chloropus

- **Length** : 32–35 cm
- **Weight** : 190–375 g
- **Food** : mainly plants, also fish and insects
- **Clutch** : 5–9 eggs (April–July)

The unobtrusive Moorhen is a common bird of lowland waters, wherever there is enough vegetation for it to hide, feed and nest. It occurs throughout most of Britain, absent only from high ground and the northern and western islands. Present throughout the year, it can easily be found on almost any lake or slow-flowing river as it crosses open water with bobbing head and flicking tail, its loud, liquid calls betraying its presence when the bird itself is hidden. Common and widespread over much of Europe, the Moorhen must be one of the most cosmopolitan species; occurring throughout most of the world.

Coot
Fulica atra

- **Length** : 36–38 cm
- **Weight** : 500 g–1.2 kg
- **Food** : aquatic vegetation and insects
- **Clutch** : 6–10 eggs (March–July)

Another very common bird, the Coot can be found throughout the year on all but the smallest lowland water bodies, especially slow-flowing rivers, lakes, reservoirs and flooded gravel-pits. Coots are widely distributed in spring when a pair's noisy, aggressive behaviour towards neighbouring Coots makes them very obvious. In winter they temporarily lose their pugnacious attitude and may congregate in large flocks, often in the company of diving ducks, on lakes and reservoirs and even in estuaries or on the sea in very hard weather. The Coot is equally widespread and common throughout much of lowland Europe wherever suitable habitat occurs.

Crane

Grus grus

After an absence of several hundred years, this very tall and very gregarious species has bred in Britain since 1981. The small group in the Norfolk Broads has slowly increased in number to around 20, with a few additional birds present in winter only. However, in order to witness the marvellous site of several hundred calling birds together, a visit to the continent is necessary. Large numbers are present at the famous Lac du Der site in the Champagne-Ardennes region of northeastern France between October and March, their numbers much increased by migrants passing through in February, March, October and November. Here, as in Les Landes south of Bordeaux and other areas where they occur regularly, they feed on waste grain in fields of harvested maize.

- **Length :** 1.1–1.2 m
- **Weight :** 3.9–7.0 kg
- **Food :** grains, shoots, insects, worms
- **Clutch :** 2 eggs (May–June)

Little Bustard

Tetrax tetrax

This is an exceedingly rare species in Britain, with only a very few lost individuals occurring from time to time. The species that used to breed on Salisbury Plain centuries ago, and has recently been reintroduced, is the related but much larger Great Bustard. Until quite recently the Little Bustard bred on much of the open agricultural land across the southern half of Europe but has declined in the face of agricultural intensification. With intense conservation efforts some relict breeding populations are still doing quite well in parts of southern and central France. Most of these birds winter in the Crau near the Camargue in the very south of France, where the species also breeds in good numbers, or move on to the Iberian peninsular. Females lack the black neck markings.

- **Length :** 40–45 cm
- **Weight :** 600–980 g
- **Food :** shoots, leaves and flowers, insects
- **Clutch :** 3–4 eggs (May–June)

Oystercatcher
Haematopus ostralegus

- **Length** : 40–45 cm
- **Weight** : 400–745 g
- **Food** : molluscs, marine and earth-worms, crabs, leatherjackets
- **Clutch** : 3 eggs (April–May)

The distinctive Oystercatcher is a shorebird of the coasts of northern Europe. In Britain it breeds most commonly along the coastline of Wales, Scotland and northern England, with smaller numbers in East Anglia and the Solent and a few others scattered elsewhere. In recent years inland breeding has become more common and takes place in much of Scotland and the very north of England as well as along many rivers and extensive wetlands further south, where it now breeds alongside Curlews and Lapwings. In winter most inland breeding birds move to the coast and especially to the larger estuaries, where they are joined by immigrants from the north.

Black-winged Stilt
Himantopus himantopus

- **Length** : 35–40 cm
- **Weight** : 140–290 g
- **Food** : aquatic insects and larvae
- **Clutch** : 4 eggs (April–May)

This is another species that is easy to identify with its bold black and white plumage and absurdly long, bright pink legs. The sexes can be separated as females have duller dark brown (not black) backs and usually have more black on the head. It is a rarity in Britain but one or two do turn up on occasions in the south of the country and may even stay for months; very occasionally they breed. A migrant that occurs commonly on some coastal areas on southern Europe between April and September, it favours saltpans and other very shallow coastal waters; it breeds inland at a few sites.

Avocet

Recurvirostra avosetta

The Avocet, with its striking pied plumage, long blue legs and upturned bill, is rare in Britain but known to most birdwatchers as the logo of the RSPB. After a long absence as a regular breeding species it has now recolonised many of the estuaries and coastal lagoons in the south of Britain after returning to breed at the RSPB's Minsmere reserve in Suffolk in 1947. It is present in Britain all year with over 60 breeding sites (most are bird reserves) south of a line from Morecambe Bay to the Wash. In winter it disperses to other nearby suitable sites; it is very rare inland. Minsmere is still a very good place to watch this very attractive bird. It can be quite common at suitable sites on the coasts of the southern two-thirds of Europe.

- **Length :** 42–45 cm
- **Weight :** 220–435 g
- **Food :** small saltwater crustaceans and worms
- **Clutch :** 3–4 eggs (April–May)

Little Ringed Plover

Charadrius dubius

A relatively recent arrival in Britain as a regular breeding species, the ever-active Little Ringed Plover is very similar to the slightly larger and more coastal Ringed Plover. It first bred here at Tring in 1938 and since then has exploited the proliferation of suitable habitat provided at large gravel pits and other man-made sites throughout much of lowland Britain. It is a migrant occurring between March and September, particularly common on the open shores of gravel pits and reservoirs in the Midlands and Home Counties. However, don't expect to find it easily, it is an unobtrusive species which blends in well with its preferred habitat of bare gravel or sandy shores and never occurs in large numbers.

- **Length :** 14–15 cm
- **Weight :** 30–55 g
- **Food :** insects, spiders, worms
- **Clutch :** 4 eggs (April–May)

Ringed Plover
Charadrius hiaticula

Unlike its smaller cousin the Little Ringed Plover, this species is present throughout the year in Britain. It breeds around much of our shoreline, mainly on shingle and sandy beaches, but is much commoner in the west and north, especially where there is less human disturbance. Some birds now breed inland along our major rivers and on the shores of large gravel pits. In winter it occurs along much of the British coastline, being particularly numerous on the major estuaries where numbers are increased by birds from breeding grounds farther north. It occurs at many inland sites during both spring and autumn migrations.

- **Length :** 18–20 cm
- **Weight :** 35–84 g
- **Food :** insects, marine worms, small molluscs
- **Clutch :** 3–4 eggs (April–July)

Lapwing
Vanellus vanellus

The Lapwing, a lively and noisy bird with characteristic broad rectangular wings, is present in the British Isles throughout the year. Other names for this species that were used in the past include 'Green Plover', referring to the metallic green sheen of its back and wings and 'Peewit', which describes its characteristic call. A species of open agricultural land, especially wet meadows, it occurs throughout lowland Britain in all months of the year although it is now somewhat scarce in much of the far west. With intensified agriculture it has declined as a breeding species but with many birds arriving from the continent for the winter it is much more widespread and numerous between October and March.

- **Length :** 28–31 cm
- **Weight :** 130–330 g
- **Food :** insects, worms
- **Clutch :** 4 eggs (March–June)

Dunlin
Calidris alpina

This is a small, active wader. In Britain it is a scarce breeding species, almost exclusively confined to the wet moorlands of the upland areas of northern England, west Wales and the highlands and islands of Scotland. In winter, when numbers are much increased by birds from farther north, it can be found around most of our coastline, wherever there are flat open expanses of mud; it occurs in large flocks on all the larger muddy estuaries such as the Humber, Wash or Severn. It can also be seen on large inland waters with muddy edges, especially at migration times. It is similarly common in winter on larger mudflats on the Atlantic shores of mainland Europe. In winter it is a much duller, greyer bird with a white belly.

- **Length :** 16–20 cm
- **Weight :** 35–70 g
- **Food :** small marine invertebrates, insects
- **Clutch :** 4 eggs (May–July)

Snipe
Gallinago gallinago

Another smallish wader, the Snipe occurs in Britain throughout the year but is much more numerous in winter. It nests on wet moorlands and marshy meadows throughout Britain but is now extremely rare as a breeding bird in the south-east. It is commoner in suitable habitat in the north of England, parts of Wales and Ireland and much of Scotland, particularly the western and northern isles. It is quite common in freshwater marshes throughout southern Britain on migration and in winter. If disturbed it flies off in a distinctive zigzag flight, giving its characteristic loud, dry call. Alternatively, this species' methodical foraging behaviour and exquisite cryptic markings can often be appreciated at length from a hide overlooking suitable ground on a nature reserve.

- **Length :** 25–27 cm
- **Weight :** 75–180 g
- **Food :** insects, worms, small molluscs
- **Clutch :** 4 eggs (April–May)

Black-tailed Godwit
Limosa limosa

A long-legged wader with a straight, long bill, the Black-tailed Godwit is quite colourful in breeding plumage. However only very small numbers nest in Britain each year; in the northern Isles (birds of the Icelandic race) and in wet meadows in parts of eastern England (birds of the continental race). In winter it is much less colourful but commoner, occurring on many of the southern estuaries, particularly the Stour, Dee, Ribble and Solent. It usually occurs further inland than the very similar Bar-tailed Godwit, which breeds much farther north in Europe, often on salt marshes and flooded meadows. Its white rump and wing-bars separate it from the plainer Bar-tailed. Good numbers pass through Britain on migration.

- **Length** : 40–44 cm
- **Weight** : 160–390 g
- **Food** : worms, molluscs, insects
- **Clutch** : 3–4 eggs (April–May)

Curlew
Numenius arquata

A large all-brown wader, the Curlew's most noticable feature is its very long down-curved bill. Its pleasant, evocative bubbling song, given in flight, is a familiar sound of the moorlands and rough pasture of the west and north of the country; unfortunately as a breeding bird it has disappeared from much of the south and east of Britain. In winter it is much commoner with birds occurring along most of our coastline, especially on the mudflats of the larger estuaries (Wash and Morecambe Bay); smaller numbers occupy inland wetlands. Many of these birds are from breeding grounds in north and east Europe and beyond.

- **Length** : 50–60 cm
- **Weight** : 500 g–1.3 kg
- **Food** : worms, molluscs, insects
- **Clutch** : 4 eggs (March–May)

Redshank
Tringa totanus

This is a smallish wader with bright orange-red legs and a ringing alarm call that has earned it the local name of 'warden of the marsh'. It breeds over much of Britain, either on salt marshes along the coast, on unimproved rough wet meadows or on moorland. The improvement of meadows in southern Britain due to modern agricultural practices has been responsible for a marked decline in numbers and reduced distribution in recent years, particularly in the south and east. As with many of the waders most birds occur along the coast in winter, particularly on estuaries, and numbers are increased by the arrival of birds from the continent.

- **Length** : 27–29 cm
- **Weight** : 85–190 g
- **Food** : worms and other small animals
- **Clutch** : 4 eggs (April–May)

Common Sandpiper
Actitis hypoleucos

This is a small brown and white wader of lake shores and rivers. When seen on the ground it bobs its tail characteristically; its manner of flight is also quite characteristic with stiff, shallow wing-beats in short bursts punctuated with glides, low over the water. It is a summer migrant that breeds on many upland rivers, streams, lochs and reservoirs in the north and west of Britain. It is much rarer in winter with only a few birds present, mainly along the coast in the south and south-west of England. However, migrants are very common and one or two birds can be seen on many inland waters, ponds, gravel pits, rivers or reservoirs in the spring and autumn.

- **Length** : 19–21 cm
- **Weight** : 35–70 g
- **Food** : insects and other small animals
- **Clutch** : 4 eggs (May)

Mediterranean Gull
Larus melanocephalus

Very similar in appearance to the familiar Black-headed Gull (with blacker head and whiter wings), the Mediterranean Gull often associates with that species. A very rare visitor to Britain until quite recently, it first bred in Britain in a large Black-headed Gull colony in Hampshire in 1968. Since then the species' breeding population has increased and expanded, with most colonies along the south coast and the largest at Langstone Harbour, Hampshire. It can be seen throughout the year in Britain; in winter (when its head becomes mainly white, see photo) it is more frequent along the coasts of southern England but may occur anywhere there are large concentrations of gulls, even inland.

- **Length :** 36–38 cm
- **Weight :** 220–390 g
- **Food :** terrestrial and aquatic insects, molluscs
- **Clutch :** 3 eggs (May–June)

Black-headed Gull
Larus ridibundus

Our most familiar gull, this species might be better named the 'Dark-brown-headed Gull', and moreover it is only dark-headed during the breeding season, becoming white-headed from August to February. It breeds throughout the country, mainly on the coast in southern England but both on the coast and inland elsewhere. In winter it is abundant in much of lowland Britain, except for the far north, especially near water. It follows rivers into major towns and cities where it can be a common sight on lakes or playing fields and will even come to gardens for bread.

- **Length :** 34–37 cm
- **Weight :** 190–400 g
- **Food :** worms, insects, molluscs
- **Clutch :** 2–3 eggs (April–June)

Common Gull

Larus canus

Why this species should have the name 'Common' isn't clear as it is by no means our commonest gull. The North American name of Mew Gull, referring to its distinctive call, seems more appropriate. Although present in Britain throughout the year this species is far more widespread outside the breeding season, with the population boosted by birds from northern Europe. Small numbers can be seen throughout most lowland areas, on the coast as well as inland. As a breeding species it is found mainly in northern England, most of western Ireland and most of Scotland where a good proportion of birds breed inland; only a few breed along southern coasts.

- **Length** : 40–42 cm
- **Weight** : 300–480 g
- **Food** : worms, insects, molluscs, crustaceans
- **Clutch** : 3 eggs (May–June)

Lesser Black-backed Gull

Larus fuscus

One of the larger gulls, this handsome species has increased and changed in occurrence in recent years. It breeds in colonies throughout Britain with most birds along the northern and western coasts or at inland sites in the northern half of the country. It was once almost holy migratory, but more and more birds stay for the winter in Britain, mainly in the south, either inland or on the coast. It is now a familiar site around many large inland waters and along much of the coast so that it might well be seen during a winter visit to any of these habitats.

- **Length** : 52–67 cm
- **Weight** : 545–1050 g
- **Food** : fish, crustaceans, vegetable matter
- **Clutch** : 3 eggs (May–June)

Herring Gull
Larus argentatus

- **Length** : 55–67 cm
- **Weight** : 690 g–1.24 kg
- **Food** : small animals, vegetable matter, waste
- **Clutch** : 3 eggs (April–July)

The most familiar of the larger gulls in Britain, this is the only common large gull with pink legs and a pale grey back. A resident here, the majority of birds are found around the coast although some breed inland, especially in Scotland. They nest in large, noisy colonies on islands and cliffs; anywhere that is safe from ground predators. The population increased and expanded greatly during the 20th century as the species took advantage of man's activities; some birds now even nest on buildings, particularly in seaside towns. However, at present it appears to be declining again. In winter it is still mainly coastal with some birds at inland gravel pits and reservoirs.

Yellow-legged Gull
Larus cachinnans

- **Length** : 55–67 cm
- **Weight** : 800 g–1.5 kg
- **Food** : fish, crustaceans, vegetable matter
- **Clutch** : 3 eggs (March–June)

Until quite recently the Yellow-legged Gull was considered a race of Herring Gull and was widely known as the Mediterranean Herring Gull, as it replaces the Herring Gull as the common large gull in southern Europe. It is very similar to the Herring Gull, differing most notably in the colour of its legs (which are bright yellow not pink) but there are other more subtle differences too; it has a different wing-tip pattern and a darker grey back. It is a rare species in Britain, with just a few pairs breeding mainly in the south, but it is more widespread and numerous outside of the breeding season.

Great Black-backed Gull

Larus marinus

The largest gull and more closely associated with the sea than other larger species, the Great Black-backed Gull can be identified by its large size, black back (usually very dark grey in Lesser Black-backed) and pinkish legs. It breeds mainly on the western and northern coasts of the British Isles though birds may be present in summer on the east or south coasts. In winter it is more widespread and numerous, present in small numbers at many inland sites, especially large reservoirs and gravel pits. Unlike other gulls it is not a particularly gregarious species, even breeding colonies usually number just a few pairs.

- **Length :** 64–78 cm
- **Weight :** 1.2–2.3 kg
- **Food :** fish, crustaceans, molluscs
- **Clutch :** 2–3 eggs (April–July)

Kittiwake

Rissa tridactyla

This charming species is a true 'sea' gull, seldom seen far from the coast. The name describes its call well; its screeching *kittee-wa-aaake* call a characteristic sound of spring at many sea-cliffs in northern and western Britain. There are very large numbers of birds in many of these colonies. Bempton Cliffs in Yorkshire has one of the largest and there are a few small colonies farther south on the east coast and on the south coast, often on buildings such as dock warehouses or piers. From September to March colonies are empty with all birds at sea, where they roost. With autumn westerly gales a few birds get blown inland, turning up on gravel pits and reservoirs.

- **Length :** 38–40 cm
- **Weight :** 300–520 g
- **Food :** marine invertebrates and small fish
- **Clutch :** 2 eggs (May–July)

Sandwich Tern
Sterna sandvicensis

- **Length :** 36–41 cm
- **Weight :** 215–290 g
- **Food :** small marine fish
- **Clutch :** 2 eggs (April–July)

Like all the terns, this species is a summer visitor that often breeds in very large colonies. It is very much a coastal species with colonies distributed around much of the British coastline. As with all terns it nests of the ground, often on sand or shingle around islands where there are few ground predators. It also suffers from disturbance and has declined over the last century as its preferred beaches were taken over by human interests. Today most colonies are on nature reserves where human access is strictly controlled.

Common Tern
Sterna hirundo

- **Length :** 31–35 cm
- **Weight :** 80–175 g
- **Food :** small fish, some crustaceans
- **Clutch :** 1–3 eggs (May–July)

This is our most familiar tern, although not the most numerous despite its name. It breeds in many sites in southern Britain, but is somewhat replaced by a very similar species in the north, the Arctic Tern. Small breeding colonies occur along the coast and also at many inland sites nowadays as they often colonise larger gravel pits and reservoirs. Favourite sand or gravel islands are soon overgrown, often flooded or trampled by Canada Geese at many sites (especially on nature reserves) these problems have been overcome by the provision of nesting rafts. Today the harsh, excited cries of the Common Tern are now quite familiar around water bodies in many parts of Britain.

Little Tern

Sterna albifrons

The smallest tern and one of the smallest seabirds, this species returns from Africa in April to nest in small isolated colonies around our coast. It nests on sand or shingle beaches, which makes it very vulnerable to human disturbance, but it can do well in sites where adequate protection is afforded; people kept away and predators controlled. The best areas are the coasts in the Hebrides, around the Solent and in East Anglia with several colonies in Ireland and North Wales and other isolated ones elsewhere. It is widespread but not very common on the continent; good numbers nest on islands along the Loire river in France.

- **Length :** 22–24 cm
- **Weight :** 50–65 g
- **Food :** small fish, crustaceans and insects
- **Clutch :** 2–3 eggs (April–July)

Rock Dove

Columba livia

This is the ancestor of the domestic pigeon, which is in turn the ancestor of all street or feral pigeons. Wild Rock Doves are difficult to differentiate from feral pigeons as they readily interbreed, and therefore little is known of the lives of 'real' Rock Doves. Feral pigeons breed almost everywhere in Britain but populations of apparently fairly pure wild Rock Doves occur on the west and north coasts of Scotland, the Hebrides, Shetland and the west coast of Ireland. Here they nest in sea caves and cliff crevices and feed on the cliff tops and nearby fields. Look for the white rump and double black wing bar.

- **Length :** 31–34 cm
- **Weight :** 235–370 g
- **Food :** especially seeds, snails, worms
- **Clutch :** 2 eggs (April–October)

Stock Dove
Columba oenas

- **Length** : 32–34 cm
- **Weight** : 240–360 g
- **Food** : especially seeds, some insects
- **Clutch** : 2 eggs (March–August)

This is one of those species that seems to go about its life unnoticed by most people. It inhabits areas of open woodland, farmland with scattered trees and large parks. It nests in a hole in a tree; in some areas where these aren't present it will make do with a hole in the wall of an unoccupied building, or even a rabbit burrow. A quite widespread resident of farming areas of the British Isles, it is absent from upland areas and much of Scotland and Ireland but is quite common in much of England and Wales despite recent declines due to the use of herbicides. Another cause of its decline may be a reduction in nest sites in the aftermath of Dutch elm disease.

Woodpigeon
Columba palumbus

- **Length** : 40–42 cm
- **Weight** : 460–570 g
- **Food** : seeds, buds, insects
- **Clutch** : 1–2 eggs (March–September)

The Woodpigeon is surely one of our most familiar birds, nesting not only in farmland but also in woodland, parks, gardens and virtually any urban green space with trees. It occurs everywhere except the very far north and west of Scotland and on very high ground. Recent population increases have been linked to an increase and extension in the planting of oilseed rape. It is mainly resident in Britain with a few birds moving south in winter. It is common on the continent; very large flocks can be seen migrating in autumn as huge numbers of northern breeding birds move south for the winter.

Collared Dove

Streptopelia decaocto

The Collared Dove is a newcomer to our shores. It probably arrived in Europe around 1900, spreading naturally from Asia. It first bred in Britain, in Norfolk, in 1955; since then it has invaded almost the whole country and is now a very common garden bird. The reasons for its rapid expansion are unknown, although many theories have been advanced including changes in climate and agricultural practices. It is sedentary and occurs throughout most of Britain wherever there are gardens, parks and cultivated areas, avoiding uplands and sparsely populated islands. Its simple trisyllabic crooning call can be heard in most months of the year.

- **Length :** 31–33 cm
- **Weight :** 125–240 g
- **Food :** seeds, berries, buds
- **Clutch :** 2 eggs (March–October)

Turtle Dove

Streptopelia turtur

This beautifully marked migrant dove occurs in cultivated rural areas of Britain between April and October. It feeds mainly on weed seeds and prefers warm, dry, lowland arable land, so only breeds in the south and east of England and rarely if ever reaches Wales, Scotland and Ireland. Recent population and distribution declines may well be due to agricultural intensification, although the shooting (both legal and illegal) of birds on migration through parts of Iberia and south-west France is surely not helping the situation. Nevertheless, it is still a common bird in rural areas throughout much of the southern two-thirds of Europe.

- **Length :** 26–28 cm
- **Weight :** 100–210 g
- **Food :** seeds, berries, some insects
- **Clutch :** 1–2 eggs (May–August)

Cuckoo
Cuculus canorus

- **Length** : 32–34 cm
- **Weight** : 90–160 g
- **Food** : insects (especially hairy caterpillars)
- **Clutch** : 8–12 eggs (April–July)

Nearly everybody knows the male Cuckoo's call, but it is surprisingly hard to see. The Cuckoo is a famous harbinger of spring but is also infamous as a brood parasite, laying its eggs in the nests of other species. It is a relatively common and widespread migrant to much of Britain, being commoner where its main host species are most abundant. In the west of Scotland and Ireland and Wales the most frequent host is the Meadow Pipit, while in central, eastern and southern England Dunnocks and Reed Warblers are the favoured hosts. Cuckoos are common and widespread on the continent.

Barn Owl
Tyto alba

- **Length** : 33–35 cm
- **Weight** : 60–135 g
- **Food** : small rodents, a few birds
- **Clutch** : 6–9 eggs (April–October)

The beautiful Barn Owl has a patchy distribution over much of the British Isles, occurring in areas of rough grazing where appropriate nest sites are present; mainly in the lofts of old farm buildings and hollow trees. It has declined sharply in the past due to persecution, pesticide poisoning and road casualties but has recently started to increase again thanks to more responsible farming practices and the provision of suitable nest boxes. It feeds mainly at night, flying over meadows, heath, light scrub and along roadside verges, looking for voles. In summer, when nights are short and there are owlets to feed, Barn Owls are easier to find as they often begin to hunt before dusk.

Scops Owl

Otus scops

Only a very rare vagrant to Britain, the diminutive Scops Owl is a migrant coming to breed in warm, dry areas of southern Europe; in the very south some birds are resident. It feeds almost exclusively on large insects and favours areas where these are abundant, such as fallow land, open scrub and vineyards. It roosts in trees during the day and nests in tree holes, although it will also nest in holes in walls and readily takes to nest boxes. Around the Mediterranean in summer listen for its distinctive song, a *tyuh* note repeated every few seconds; it can often be heard in small towns. Be careful though, as the Midwife Toad makes a very similar sound.

- **Length :** 19–20 cm
- **Weight :** 60–135 g
- **Food :** large insects and other small animals
- **Clutch :** 4–5 eggs (April–June)

Little Owl

Athene noctua

Britain's smallest owl, this species is often quite active during the day. It is not a native species; birds were deliberately released at various sites in England during the second half of the 19th century and by the 1930s the species had colonised much of England. It is absent from Ireland, much of west Wales, northern Scotland and south-west England. It prefers open country with ample hedgerows, copses, orchards or woodland. Although it has declined recently, partly to poisoning through the use of pesticides, this decline may well now have slowed or stopped. It is widespread and fairly common over much of the southern two-thirds of Europe.

- **Length :** 21–23 cm
- **Weight :** 140–200 g
- **Food :** worms and large insects
- **Clutch :** 3–5 eggs (April–June)

Tawny Owl
Strix aluco

- **Length :** 37–39 cm
- **Weight :** 330–570 g
- **Food :** small mammals and birds
- **Clutch :** 2–5 eggs (February–April)

The hooting of our common woodland owl is relatively well known; but the bird itself isn't very often seen. It occurs throughout Britain in woodland, even in parks and large gardens as long as there are some big trees, and in farmland with copses or overgrown hedgerows with trees. It is absent from Ireland and very scarce in the north of Scotland but has increased there with extensive forestry plantation. There are recent signs that the population is in decline; this may well be due to birds being poisoned by the use of new types of rodenticides. It is common and widely distributed over most of Europe. It is sedentary by nature, and is most vocal in late winter and early spring.

Long-eared Owl
Asio otus

- **Length :** 35–37 cm
- **Weight :** 220–370 g
- **Food :** small mammals, birds
- **Clutch :** 3–5 eggs (March–May)

Not a common bird in Britain, this beautiful owl's secretive habits make it all the more difficult to see, although with luck you may find one or more (they form communal roosts in winter) sitting stiffly upright against the trunk of a conifer or deep in a dense, scrubby thicket. It has a scattered distribution during the breeding season with more birds in the east and very few in the west (with the same pattern repeated in Ireland); distribution is similar in winter but numbers increase with the arrival of birds from northern Europe. The related Short-eared Owl is paler with yellow eyes and smaller ear-tufts, and is active in the daytime.

Swift
Apus apus

An extremely common and visible species, the Swift spends nearly all of its life in the air, only touching down to nest, for which it uses cavities in high buildings. In Britain it arrives back from Africa in late April and leaves again in July and August. During summer screaming parties of cavorting Swifts are a common sight of many villages and towns in Britain; it is only absent from the far north and upland areas. Swifts feed solely on flying insects and will travel long distances to find good concentrations of them. Also common on the continent, both here and there numbers may increase with the recent inclusion of integral Swift nest-boxes in the construction of new high-rise buildings.

- **Length** : 16–17 cm
- **Weight** : 30–55 g
- **Food** : small flying insects
- **Clutch** : 2–3 eggs (May–July)

Alpine Swift
Tachymarptis melba

This species looks like a giant Swift with the markings of a Sand Martin; its long, drawn-out twittering call is quite distinctive too. Only rarely seen in Britain. it is a species of rocky Mediterranean coasts and high-altitude cliffs in southern Europe. It constructs its nest in crevices and holes on sea-cliffs around the coast and on inland cliffs and tall buildings. It is nowhere very common; look for it in any suitable habitat between April and September. The species appears to be nomadic with breeding sites often occupied for only a few seasons.

- **Length** : 20–22 cm
- **Weight** : 75–125 g
- **Food** : aerial insects and spiders
- **Clutch** : 3–5 eggs (April–June)

Kingfisher

Alcedo atthis

T he brightly coloured Kingfisher is surely one of Britain's most popular birds. It feeds on small fish, which it catches in clean rivers, canals, gravel pits and reservoirs throughout England and Wales. It occurs locally in Ireland and just a few pairs breed in Scotland, in the very south. It needs open water to feed, so in winter birds breeding in upland areas tend to move to lower ground and there is a marked movement to the coast, birds becoming more common around estuaries. Many may starve in very severe winters, when lakes freeze over for days at a time. Recent efforts to clean our waterways and the impact of global warming may well help this species to increase.

- **Length :** 16–17 cm
- **Weight :** 34–46 g
- **Food :** small fish, aquatic insects
- **Clutch :** 6–7 eggs (April–August)

Bee-eater

Merops apiaster

T he very colourful Bee-eater is on the increase. It is a summer visitor to southern Europe, present from May to August, frequenting warm open areas with trees and hedges and an abundance of large insects; it typically nests in holes excavated in riverbanks. A few birds turn up in Britain each spring and once in a while a pair stays to breed; there have been three such attempts since 2000. This species experiences fluctuating periods of range contraction and expansion; at present on the near continent the tendency is of an overall increase and northerly expansion and the species is not at all rare in the centre of France and even around Paris. With global warming it may soon be a regular British breeding species.

- **Length :** 27–29 cm
- **Weight :** 50–80 g
- **Food :** bees, wasps, dragonflies
- **Clutch :** 6–7 eggs (May–June)

Roller
Coracias garrulus

The colourful Roller is about the size of a Jackdaw. It is a summer visitor to warm areas of southern and central Europe, and is a very infrequent visitor to Britain. Its European range has been decreasing for a long time; it has recently disappeared from several countries including Germany, Latvia, Slovakia, Austria, the Czech Republic and Slovenia. Changes in agricultural practises, with much more intensive rearing of livestock, may be part of the problem. The Roller is strongly territorial with each pair inhabiting a large area, so it is never a very numerous species. However, it perches in the open, on wires and dead branches, so where it is present it can be quite easy to locate.

- **Length :** 30–32 cm
- **Weight :** 110–190 g
- **Food :** mainly insects, sometimes small lizards
- **Clutch :** 3–5 eggs (June–July)

Hoopoe
Upupa epops

There can hardly be an easier bird to identify that the Hoopoe, with its bright pink, black and white plumage, long, curved bill and erectile crest, along with its very characteristic *poup-poup-poup* song. Yet despite this it can be surprisingly difficult to see. Small numbers arrive in Britain each year, having 'overshot' their breeding grounds further south in Europe. They arrive in Europe from Africa in March or April and leave in August and September, inhabiting open areas with trees or walls to provide breeding sites. Hoopoes have probably suffered from agricultural intensification but are still common in the southern two-thirds of Europe, especially in Spain.

- **Length :** 26–28 cm
- **Weight :** 40–100 g
- **Food :** insects and their larvae, other small animals
- **Clutch :** 6–8 eggs (March–July)

Green Woodpecker
Picus viridis

O f the three species of woodpecker that occur in Britain, this is the largest and least confined to woodland. It is colourful and easy to identify with its green plumage, bright yellow rump, black and red on markings on the head and loud, laughing call. It inhabits mature deciduous woodland, parkland, heaths and commons where it nests in a hole excavated in a large tree. Green woodpeckers feed more in the open than other woodpeckers, often searching for ants and other insects on grassland, meadows or lawns. It is resident and common in much of southern England wherever there is mature woodland, much more localised in the north and in southern Scotland and absent from Ireland (which has no woodpeckers).

- **Length :** 31–33 cm
- **Weight :** 140–190 g
- **Food :** ants and other insects
- **Clutch :** 5–7 eggs (April–June)

Great Spotted Woodpecker
Dendrocopos major

T he commonest and most widespread of British woodpeckers, this species is probably also the best known as it readily visits bird tables so long as they are within easy reach of trees. It inhabits both deciduous and coniferous woodland throughout Britain, but is scarcer and more locally distributed in the north and absent from many northern and western islands and Ireland. British birds are resident, a few extra birds arrive for the winter from northern Europe. Numbers have increased recently thanks to the increase in dead trees as a result of Dutch elm disease, more enlightened forestry practices and garden feeding. It is a common and widespread species on the continent.

- **Length :** 22–23 cm
- **Weight :** 70–100 g
- **Food :** insects, larvae, seeds
- **Clutch :** 4–7 eggs (April–June)

Lesser Spotted Woodpecker

Dendrocopos minor

This species appears to have a lot of problems in Britain, and the reasons for its decline are little understood. It is a very small bird that occurs in mature broadleaved woods and usually forages high in the tree-tops, making it very difficult to find, especially in Britain where it is confined to the woodlands of south-eastern England with lower numbers in the Midlands and parts of northern England and Wales. On the continent its loud *kee, kee, kee, kee* calls can be quite commonly heard wherever large broadleaved trees occur; not only in woodland but also in overgrown hedgerows and even gardens as long as they have some large trees. The crown of the female is black, not red.

- **Length :** 14–15 cm
- **Weight :** 15–25 g
- **Food :** wood-boring insect larvae caterpillars
- **Clutch :** 4–6 eggs (April–July)

Crested Lark

Galerida cristata

Although it is common just across the Channel, this stocky, short-tailed and long-crested lark is a vanishingly rare visitor to Britain. It is widespread and relatively common on the continent, wherever there is unvegetated, dry open ground. Its natural habitat is semi-desert, which it finds throughout much of the Mediterranean area. It has, however taken to similar situations in man-made sites and can be found quite commonly in such areas as railway sidings, little-used aerodromes, supermarket car parks, industrial estates or large farm yards. Recent declines and range contraction have been attributed to agricultural intensification, but largely remain a mystery.

- **Length :** 17 cm
- **Weight :** 38–52 g
- **Food :** seeds, leaves, insects and worms
- **Clutch :** 3–5 eggs (March–July)

Skylark
Alauda arvensis

Once an abundant species on lowland farming areas, the Skylark has recently undergone a massive decline in numbers in Britain and on much of the continent. However, despite these losses it is still a very widespread species, breeding throughout the British Isles and common in open country almost everywhere. Many birds move to lower ground for the winter when the population increases with immigrants from northern Europe. Recent conservation research work has shown that the Skylark and intensive farming are not incompatible, but simple changes in agricultural practices may mean that the singing Skylark, high in the sky, will remain a common sight in Britain and throughout Europe.

- **Length :** 18–19 cm
- **Weight :** 30–55 g
- **Food :** seeds, leaves, insects (summer)
- **Clutch :** 3–5 eggs (April–July)

Sand Martin
Riparia riparia

This small brown-and-white martin is one of the earliest summer migrants to return to Britain from Africa. Birds breed together in large colonies, digging burrows in vertical banks along rivers and in the sides of gravel and sand pits. It is very widespread in Britain with colonies as far north as Orkney, but has a patchy distribution due to lack of nesting sites in many areas. On migration birds gather wherever there is an expanse of water. It has recently declined alarmingly, probably due to drought conditions on its wintering grounds in the Sahel region of Africa in some years. A common and widespread species on the continent, it is especially numerous in Spain.

- **Length :** 12 cm
- **Weight :** 11–15 g
- **Food :** small flying insects
- **Clutch :** 4–6 eggs (May–July)

Crag Martin
Ptyonoprogne rupestris

The Crag Martin is a large, dark martin with no distinctive markings except for the white spots in the tail, which are often only visible at short range and in good light. It's a bird of the very south of Europe that is an extremely rare vagrant to Britain. It nests on cliffs and rocky outcrops in mountains and in places along the Mediterranean coast. Northern birds are migratory but most individuals are sedentary – it is the only member of the swallow family that occurs in Mediterranean areas in winter. The nearest colonies to Britain are those to the north of the Massif Central, near Clerment Ferrand.

- **Length :** 14.5 cm
- **Weight :** 17–27 g
- **Food :** small flying insects
- **Clutch :** 3–5 eggs (May–July)

Swallow
Hirundo rustica

The Swallow is a popular and well-known species which often nests in farm buildings, particularly where livestock are present. A long-distance migrant, it arrives in Britain in April and leaves again for Africa in October. It breeds almost everywhere, even in Shetland, but is much more common in lowland farming areas. There has been a decline in numbers which can be attributed to a decrease in the distribution of farm livestock (Swallows feed on the insects attracted to and disturbed by grazing livestock) and loss of nesting sites as traditional farm outbuildings are demolished or converted. It is a common species almost everywhere on the continent.

- **Length :** 17–19 cm
- **Weight :** 16–24 g
- **Food :** small flying insects
- **Clutch :** 4–5 eggs (May–August)

House Martin
Delichon urbicum

- **Length :** 12.5 cm
- **Weight :** 13–23 g
- **Food :** small flying insects
- **Clutch :** 3–5 eggs (May–August)

This very distinctive species has a striking white rump, and is known for its cup-shaped mud nest that it builds under the eaves of houses. It is a migrant, usually arriving and departing a little later than the Swallow and Sand Martin. It is as widespread in Britain as the other two species, with birds breeding in Shetland some years, and is most numerous in the south of England and Wales and in the west of Ireland. As with many other species there has been a recent decline due to a shortage of the flying insects it eats. Another cause particular to this species may be a lack of muddy puddles, needed as a supply of nest building material; birds can carry the wet mud only a short distance. It is common and widespread in Europe.

Meadow Pipit
Anthus pratensis

- **Length :** 14.5 cm
- **Weight :** 14–23 g
- **Food :** all kinds of small insects
- **Clutch :** 3–5 eggs (April–July)

Pipits are small, plain-coloured ground-dwelling birds. Several different species occur in Britain, some of which breed; the Meadow Pipit is the commonest. It breeds throughout Britain in upland rough grassland, young forestry plantations, heathland, salt marsh and rough ground; at this time it is much more numerous in the north and west. For the winter many birds move to lower land and to the south; the British population is also augmented by birds from northern Europe. An overall decline in numbers is due to agricultural intensification and increased use of marginal land. The Meadow Pipit occurs throughout the northern half of Europe.

Yellow Wagtail

Motacilla flava

There are several races of the Yellow Wagtail which vary mainly in the colour of their heads and in distribution, they are all migrants wintering in Africa and breeding in Europe and Asia. Most of the birds breeding in Britain have a green crown and cheeks, and yellow chin and eyebrows. The Blue-headed Wagtail (photo and illustration) breeds on the near continent, and a few reach Britain each year. Confusing intergrades between the two are not infrequent. This species breeds in most of lowland England, wherever there are large areas of flooded grassland and water meadows, but its range has retracted recently. Habitat loss through drainage is one of the main problems.

- **Length :** 17 cm
- **Weight :** 14–20 g
- **Food :** insects, spiders, worms
- **Clutch :** 4–6 eggs (May–July)

Grey Wagtail

Motacilla cinerea

This handsome, active, very long-tailed bird is a familiar sight on fast-flowing rivers and streams throughout much of western and northern Britain. As with all wagtails the Grey Wagtail wags its tail but in this species its excessively long tail accentuates the impression. Many birds move to lower ground or south for the winter and at this time birds can turn up in areas where they don't breed, including city centres. A species that's increasing in range and numbers in Britain, it is common and widespread on the continent. Females lack the black throat and juveniles are duller, but all show the vivid yellow undertail.

- **Length :** 18–19 cm
- **Weight :** 14–25 g
- **Food :** mainly insects, small molluscs
- **Clutch :** 4–6 eggs (April–July)

White Wagtail
Motacilla alba alba

- **Length :** 17–18 cm
- **Weight :** 16–25 g
- **Food :** insects, spiders, seeds
- **Clutch :** 5–6 eggs (April–July)

The Pied and White Wagtails are two different races of the same species. The White Wagtail is the continental and much more widespread form. Both races are readily identified by their having black and white plumage with characteristic white face, the latter particularly apparent in the nesting season. Adult birds of the two forms are not too difficult to separate, the White having a grey back and rump that contrasts with the black of the rest of the plumage. Young birds are much harder to separate. Migrant White Wagtails pass through Britain each year and they are very easy to see on the continent, especially near lakes, rivers, reservoirs and canals.

Pied Wagtail
Motacilla alba yarrellii

- **Length :** 17–18 cm
- **Weight :** 16–25 g
- **Food :** insects, spiders, seeds
- **Clutch :** 5–6 eggs (April–July)

This is the British version of the White Wagtail, which breeds almost exclusively in Britain with just a few pairs on the near continent, in France, Belgium and particularly Holland. It is easily identified as it is the only black and white bird that walks on the ground, constantly wagging its tail. Young birds can be more confusing as they are much less boldly marked, but their habitats and behaviour are like the adults. It occurs throughout Britain (although it is much more numerous in the north and west) almost anywhere but particularly near water and is quite confiding, sometimes nesting in buildings and even in bird-watching hides where they overlook wet areas.

Dipper
Cinclus cinclus

A dumpy bird of fast-flowing, clear streams and rivers, with a characteristic white bib and bobbing action when perched on a rock in the middle of the water. It forages for its insect prey in the water, readily submerging completely and walking on the stream bed or allowing itself to be carried on the currents. It occurs in suitable habitat throughout the north and west of the British Isles, being particularly common in south Wales, northern England and south-east Scotland; it occurs locally in Ireland. There is some concern that numbers may be declining, perhaps because of pollution and acidification of rivers due to conifer planting.

- **Length :** 18 cm
- **Weight :** 53–76 g
- **Food :** insects and aquatic larvae
- **Clutch :** 4–5 eggs (March–May)

Wren
Troglodytes troglodytes

A small bird with a big voice and a short, often cocked tail; if it wasn't for its remarkably loud song this secretive little brown bird would often go unnoticed. It is one of the most widespread and commonest of resident British birds, occurring almost everywhere, even on the remotest islands although it does avoid very high ground. A secretive life hides some quite interesting habits. Males will build several nests before the female chooses one of them (normally the best hidden) to lay her eggs and in woodland sites males are often polygamous. It is equally common and widespread on the continent.

- **Length :** 9–10 cm
- **Weight :** 7–11 g
- **Food :** insects, small spiders
- **Clutch :** 5–8 eggs (April–July)

Dunnock
Prunella modularis

- **Length :** 14.5 cm
- **Weight :** 16–25 g
- **Food :** insects, seeds (winter)
- **Clutch :** 4–6 eggs (April–July)

Another unobtrusive resident species, the Dunnock goes about its life often unnoticed by all but the most observant. It is most obvious in the spring when the male gives its quite musical song from an exposed perch; otherwise they scuttle about in the bottoms of hedgerows and under bushes, constantly searching for food. It has a fascinating private life, with both sexes sometimes polygamous. It is common and widespread throughout most of lowland Britain, breeding as far north as Orkney in farmland with hedgerows, woodland edges, scrub, parks and gardens. Recent population declines in some areas may have been caused by the destruction of hedgerows. It occurs throughout Europe except for the far south.

Robin
Erithacus rubecula

- **Length :** 14 cm
- **Weight :** 14–23 g
- **Food :** insects, worms, grubs fruit
- **Clutch :** 4–6 eggs (April–July)

Widespread and common, confiding (even sitting on the garden spade), distinctively coloured, a competent songster and immortalised on countless Christmas cards, who doesn't know and like the Robin? It is one of Britain's most widespread species, occurring wherever there are bushes for nesting and damp ground for feeding; it even attempts to breed in treeless Shetland every so often. Most British Robins are resident but upland birds move to lower ground for the winter. On the continent it is often much more migratory, many birds from northern Europe moving through Britain to reach wintering grounds in Spain and Portugal.

Nightingale
Luscinia megarhynchos

A migrant that's present in Britain from April to September, this species is renowned for its singing but is hard to see well. Its loud, very musical song is given from deep in undergrowth during the night as well as by day; it is one of the few birds to sing at night. In Britain it breeds south-east of a line between the Severn and the Humber but has recently undergone a severe decline in both range and numbers. This decline is thought to be due to lack of suitable habitat; it needs dense low scrub and the presence of introduced deer in the south of the country is apparently much reducing this type of cover. It is common and widespread in southern Europe.

- **Length :** 16.5 cm
- **Weight :** 17–36 g
- **Food :** insects, spiders, worms, some berries
- **Clutch :** 4–5 eggs (May–June)

Bluethroat
Luscinia svecica

This magnificent migrant breeds locally in Europe and winters in Africa. There are various different forms, some males have red in the centre of their blue throats, others have white. Females are duller. Migrants turn up on the east coast of Britain each spring and autumn; birds of the red-spotted form have very occasionally bred in the north of Britain. The populations of the white spotted form in Belgium and the Netherlands and a smaller version on the Atlantic coast of France are expanding and increasing, maybe they will breed in the south of England eventually. They occur in rank vegetation, usually near water; the edges of gravel pits with areas of willow and reed are popular.

- **Length :** 14 cm
- **Weight :** 13–23 g
- **Food :** especially insects, some seeds and berries
- **Clutch :** 5–6 eggs (April–June)

Black Redstart
Phoenicurus ochruros

- **Length :** 14.5 cm
- **Weight :** 14–18 g
- **Food :** insects, fruits, seeds
- **Clutch :** 4–6 eggs (April–July)

The Black Redstart has been breeding in Britain in very small numbers since the early 20th century, firstly on cliffs on the south and east coasts, then in cities after bombing during World War II created suitable habitat. Nowadays it breeds here and there in England, mainly at industrial sites; there are only a few tens of pairs each year and the population may be in decline. It is common and widespread throughout much of the southern two-thirds of Europe, its scratchy little song commonly heard in rural villages, around farm buildings and large monuments and on rocky slopes. Most birds in the north of its range move farther south in Europe for the winter. Females have red tails but are otherwise grey-brown.

Redstart
Phoenicurus phoenicurus

- **Length :** 14 cm
- **Weight :** 10–20 g
- **Food :** insects, spiders, some berries
- **Clutch :** 5–7 eggs (May–June)

The Redstart is a summer migrant, present in Europe from April to September. The male is very distinctively coloured with a pleasant song. On the continent they breed in various types of wooded habitat: deciduous or evergreen woodland, well wooded river valleys, parks and large gardens, but in Britain most birds nest in upland oakwoods, being particularly common in Wales, Scotland and the north and south-west of England; they are absent from Ireland. Many migrants pass through Britain between northern Europe and Africa when they are particularly common along the east coast but can occur anywhere. They are common and widespread in suitable habitat across Europe. They will occasionally use open-fronted nest-boxes.

Whinchat
Saxicola rubetra

The smart little Whinchat is a summer migrant to much of Europe from April to September. It is an inhabitant of rough, wet grassland, and has declined quite markedly in recent times, probably as a result of 'improved' farming methods including land drainage and earlier cutting of hay. However, it is still quite a familiar bird north of a line from the Severn to the Humber and central parts of Ireland, preferring upland areas. Its presence is often given away by its scolding alarm call, delivered from the top of a tall plant or on a fence post. It is locally common in much of Europe except for the very south. Females and juveniles are duller but all have a broad pale eyebrow.

- **Length** : 12.5 cm
- **Weight** : 14–22 g
- **Food** : insects, spiders, seeds
- **Clutch** : 5–6 eggs (April–July)

Stonechat
Saxicola torquatus

A resident species in Britain, the Stonechat is not especially common or widespread. The male is a very smart bird in breeding plumage with black head and back, orange breast and white collar and wing bar. Females are duller. Stonechats often choose a prominent perch, the top branch of a gorse or bramble of a fence post and are thus easy to find in their favoured habitat of heathland and rough open ground with low bushes. Most breeding birds occupy the west coast of Britain and Ireland with large numbers in much of western Scotland, west Wales and the south coast of England; elsewhere they are rarer. In winter most birds move towards the coast. It is common in suitable habitat throughout southern Europe.

- **Length** : 12.5 cm
- **Weight** : 13–17 g
- **Food** : insects, spiders, seeds
- **Clutch** : 4–6 eggs (March–July)

Wheatear
Oenanthe oenanthe

This long-distance migrant arrives in Britain to breed in April, and stays until September. Like all species of wheatear it lives on the ground in very open areas, in Britain this is mainly on high, rocky ground with close-cropped grass in the hills of the west and north of Britain. A few birds breed elsewhere in the south, especially along the coast. It is quite widespread on the continent wherever there's high open ground or in the north. Migrating birds may appear almost anywhere in Britain in spring and autumn. The female lacks the male's black markings but has the striking white rump and black-and-white tail pattern.

- **Length :** 14.5–15.5 cm
- **Weight :** 18–30 g
- **Food :** insects, spiders, worms
- **Clutch :** 4–7 eggs (April–July)

Black-eared Wheatear
Oenanthe hispanica

This is a handsome black and white wheatear of the Mediterranean area. As with most migrants that breed in the south of Europe some birds do overshoot or get lost and turn up in Britain but only very rarely. Between April and October it can be found in dry open habitats, in sandy or rocky areas, open limestone hillsides, arid farmland and glades in olive groves and Holm Oak woodland. It breeds throughout Spain and in much of Portugal and the south of Italy and much of Greece. There are two colour morphs; some birds have white throats, others black. Females are browner.

- **Length :** 14.5 cm
- **Weight :** 14–26 g
- **Food :** insects, spiders, worms
- **Clutch :** 4–5 eggs (May–July)

Rock Thrush
Monticola saxatilis

The male Rock Thrush is a very handsome and colourful bird. Only a few have ever been found in Britain, so to see this superb bird it is necessary to visit one of the high mountain ranges of southern Europe. The Rock Thrush is a summer migrant, present on the breeding grounds from April to September. It occurs above the tree line on alpine slopes with bushes and rocky outcrops, usually exposed to the sun. Even in good habitat it doesn't occur in large numbers, so some searching is usually necessary. Suitable slopes around Gavarnie in the French Pyrenees are as good a searching ground as any.

- **Length :** 18.5 cm
- **Weight :** 40–65 g
- **Food :** insects, spiders, snails
- **Clutch :** 4–5 eggs (May–June)

Blackbird
Turdus merula

With a decent view it is quite difficult to mistake a male Blackbird, with its solid black plumage, elegant long-tailed shape and orange bill for any other species. The brown and mottled females and young are a little more difficult but should pose no real problem as they cross the lawn with bounding hops, looking (and listening) for worms. Blackbirds are common throughout Britain and the rest of Europe, wherever there are open spaces with bushes and trees: open woodland, forest clearings, meadows with hedgerows, parks or gardens. It isn't uncommon for birds to have some white feathers in their plumage which may cause confusion, and very occasionally all-white birds occur.

- **Length :** 24–25 cm
- **Weight :** 80–130 g
- **Food :** insects, worms berries
- **Clutch :** 3–5 eggs (March–July)

Fieldfare
Turдuѕ pilariѕ

- **Length :** 25.5 cm
- **Weight :** 80–140 g
- **Food :** worms, insects, berries
- **Clutch :** 5–6 eggs (March–June)

This large thrush is a winter visitor to Britain, its characteristic *chack-chack-chack* calls often heard between October and March as flocks roam the countryside, moving according to prevailing weather conditions. They arrive from the continent where they breed in all types of woodland and in parks and gardens over much of its northern two-thirds, in fact it is quite surprising that more don't breed here; a handful of pairs nest in the north of the country in most years. They may come to gardens, especially in hard weather, where they readily feed on apples or cotoneaster or pyracantha berries; this is a good chance to see their colourful plumage.

Song Thrush
Turдuѕ philomeloѕ

- **Length :** 23 cm
- **Weight :** 50–100 g
- **Food :** insects, snails, worms, berries
- **Clutch :** 3–5 eggs (March–July)

Not so long ago the loud repeated musical notes of the Song Thrush were a common spring sound throughout the British Isles. However, its numbers have declined alarmingly over the last 50 years and in many areas it is no longer present. The decline seems sharpest in farmland and suburban areas, which may well indicate that pesticides (including garden products for killing slugs and snails) are part of the cause. Still widespread and common in some areas, with enlightened attitudes towards garden management the Song Thrush's fortunes have recently begun to improve.

Redwing

Turdus iliacus

A small northern thrush that visits Britain in large numbers for the winter. Although superficially similar to the Song Thrush, it can be distinguished by the brick-red patch on each flank and obvious whitish eyebrow. A few pairs breed each year in the highlands of Scotland but most people are likely to see the Redwing feeding on berry-bushes and, later in winter, meadows and other open grassy areas in the company of Fieldfares and other birds in winter. There are more birds in the south-west of the country, numbers decrease farther north but it can be seen throughout most of Britain between October and April.

- **Length :** 21 cm
- **Weight :** 45–80 g
- **Food :** berries, fruits, some insects
- **Clutch :** 4 eggs (May–July)

Mistle Thrush

Turdus viscivorus

The largest thrush to breed in Britain, pairs of Mistle Thrushes hold large territories and are thus never particularly numerous. At first glance it is very similar to the smaller Song Thrush, but a good look shows it not only to be bigger but also much greyer with more rounded spots on the breast and belly. It has expanded its range considerably in the last 200 years or so; today it is found in most of Britain, being absent only from the Orkneys, Shetlands and Outer Hebrides. Some northern birds move south in winter and a few birds may arrive at this time from the continent, but most appear to be quite sedentary.

- **Length :** 27 cm
- **Weight :** 95–140 g
- **Food :** insects, worms, snails, berries
- **Clutch :** 3–5 eggs (April–June)

Reed Warbler
Acrocephalus scirpaceus

There are several species of small brown birds that habitually occur in waterside vegetation; the Reed Warbler is one of the most common and is widespread in Britain. It is a migrant, arriving from Africa in May and returning in September. It breeds throughout the south-eastern half of Britain wherever there are reedbeds, even small ones. There is a recent trend of population increase and extension with regular breeding in Ireland a recent phenomenon. The creation of gravel pits with resulting reedbeds and the proliferation of nature reserves may well have helped the Reed Warbler. Similar species include the more rufous Cetti's Warbler, and the streaky Sedge Warbler.

- **Length :** 12–13 cm
- **Weight :** 10–17 g
- **Food :** mainly insects and spiders
- **Clutch :** 4 eggs (May–July)

Melodious Warbler
Hippolais polyglotta

This species and the very similar Icterine Warbler are both long-distance migrants that arrive on their breeding grounds in Europe in May and leave in August and September; both occur in Britain as rare migrants. The Melodious Warbler occupies areas with lush vegetation that combine bushes and trees with open spaces, and is found throughout south-west Europe including most of France and Italy and all of Spain and Portugal. A few birds breed in the south of Belgium each year. It is most obvious when it sings from the top of a bush or tree; the song is a complex set of sounds including mimicry of other species.

- **Length :** 12–13 cm
- **Weight :** 10–17 g
- **Food :** insects and larvae, berries fruit
- **Clutch :** 4–5 eggs (May–July)

Subalpine Warbler

Sylvia cantillans

Asmall, colourful migrant warbler that arrives to breed in the south of Europe during April, and departs for its wintering grounds in sub-Saharan Africa during September. A few lost migrants arrive in Britain each year, but it is very rare and difficult to see. It inhabits warm, dry, Mediterranean scrubland with low bushes, occurring in the very south of France, nearly all of Spain and Portugal, Italy and the west Mediterranean islands. Young birds and females (photo) have a plumage similar to many other warblers but the smart male's grey head and brick-red throat and breast with neat white moustache make it quite distinctive.

- **Length :** 11.5–12.5 cm
- **Weight :** 9–14 g
- **Food :** small insects, larvae
- **Clutch :** 3–4 eggs (April–June)

Sardinian Warbler

Sylvia melanocephala

Ahandsome, perky Mediterranean warbler, this species is mainly sedentary, although some birds undertake short migratory movements. It is a relatively easy species to identify with its black head, white throat, grey body and striking red eye ring. It does not occur in Britain but occupies all areas with low scrub of the Mediterranean countries; the very south of France, most of Spain, Portugal, Italy and the Mediterranean islands. It is common and confiding, often found in areas of shrubs in gardens and town centres and even on large roundabout islands. Quite secretive, its presence is often given away by a characteristic rattling call. Females are greyer.

- **Length :** 12.5–14 cm
- **Weight :** 14–23 g
- **Food :** insects, spiders, berries
- **Clutch :** 3–4 eggs (April–July)

Whitethroat
Sylvia communis

The Whitethroat's scratchy song, often given in flight, used to be one of the most typical wildlife sounds of spring in rural Britain. However, it has declined markedly since the 1960s, mainly due to weather-related changes in its wintering quarters in Africa, although it remains a relatively common species over much of Britain. Present between April and September, it is most abundant in lowland areas with overgrown hedgerows and scrub (disused railway lines are much favoured) but is absent from all upland areas and much of the north of Scotland and extreme north and south of Ireland. It is common and widespread on the continent.

- **Length** : 13–15 cm
- **Weight** : 11–20 g
- **Food** : insects, spiders, berries
- **Clutch** : 5 eggs (May–July)

Garden Warbler
Sylvia borin

If ever a bird deserved the label 'little brown job', the Garden Warbler is surely it. With its brownish, unmarked plumage, retiring secretive habits and sweet but soft and somewhat monotonous song, this species often goes unnoticed. It is a long-distance migrant that arrives in Britain in May and leaves in September, breeding in thick scrub (but not in gardens – its name is misleading) in much of England, Wales and the south of Scotland; it is rare in the northern half of Scotland and throughout Ireland. It is relatively widespread and common in suitable habitat in Europe during late spring and summer.

- **Length** : 13.5–14.5 cm
- **Weight** : 12–25 g
- **Food** : insects, spiders, berries and fruit
- **Clutch** : 4–5 eggs (May–July)

Blackcap
Sylvia atricapilla

This species' name comes from the adult male, females (illustration) and young could more accurately be called 'browncaps'. Most birds are migrants, in Britain between April and September. At this time they nest throughout the southern two-thirds of Britain in areas with scrub, overgrown hedges or along woodland edges. Blackcaps are excellent songsters, very musical with a variety of phrases, and may mimic the songs or calls of other species. Some birds (of northern European origin) come to Britain for the winter and may be seen at feeding stations. As in Britain, it is common and increasing over much of Europe.

- **Length :** 13.5–14.5 cm
- **Weight :** 15–25 g
- **Food :** insects, larvae, berries
- **Clutch :** 5 eggs (April–July)

Chiffchaff
Phylloscopus collybita

Although it is thought of as a summer migrant by most British birdwatchers, every year a few Chiffchaffs spend the winter here, usually in the south in sheltered spots near water. It is one of the earliest migrants to arrive with many birds present in March occupying all kinds of woodland habitats. The specie's most characteristic feature is its song, a very obvious *chiff-chaff, chiff-chaff, chiff-chiff-chaff...* with slight variations on a very basic two-note theme. It is common in the southern two-thirds of the British Isles, scarce in many upland areas and Scotland and all but absent from the far north. It is a common breeding species throughout most of Europe.

- **Length :** 10.5–11.5 cm
- **Weight :** 6–9 g
- **Food :** small insects, caterpillars, spiders
- **Clutch :** 5–6 eggs (April–July)

Willow Warbler
Phylloscopus trochilus

- **Length :** 10.5–11.5 cm
- **Weight :** 6.5–11 g
- **Food :** especially small insects spiders, berries
- **Clutch :** 6–7 eggs (April–June)

This long-distance migrant arrives here in April and leaves in September, and is our most numerous summer visitor. It can be separated from the very similar Chiffchaff by its longer wings, stronger face markings and paler legs, but these characteristics can be hard to see. The two species' songs are, however, completely different. The Willow Warbler's sweet, descending refrain can be heard in spring wherever there's scrub and bushes with or without a few trees, often with a preference for wet areas. It is common and widespread throughout the northern half of Europe but only occurs on migration in the south.

Goldcrest
Regulus regulus

- **Length :** 8–10 cm
- **Weight :** 5–6 g
- **Food :** small insects, spiders
- **Clutch :** 8–10 eggs (April–July)

The tiny Goldcrest is relatively widespread and common over the whole of Britain and Europe, wherever conifers occur. Often difficult to find, in the breeding season males give their cheerful high-pitched song hidden towards the top of a conifer, in winter it is often their frequently given high-pitched calls that attract attention. Unfortunately, both song and call are very difficult to hear for many people in which case searching for this confiding species can be time-consuming. Birds breeding in northern Europe move south for the winter. Migrants arrive in October on the east coast of England, sometimes in very large numbers.

Firecrest

Regulus ignicapilla

Along with the Goldcrest, the Firecrest is Europe's smallest bird and many birdwatchers agree it is is one of the most beautiful. Once rare here, the Firecrest has gradually colonised the south of Britain since it was first proved to have bred here in 1962, in the New Forest. It is still, however, very uncommon. Most breeding birds are found in woodland with conifers in the south-east of England. It is probably easier to find in winter when individuals can be found in sheltered scrub and woodland edges along much of the south coast and a few other coastal areas (the North Wales coast is another good area) where it often follows mixed tit flocks.

- **Length** : 8–9 cm
- **Weight** : 4–5.5 g
- **Food** : small insects, spiders
- **Clutch** : 7–11 eggs (April–July)

Spotted Flycatcher

Muscicapa striata

Despite its dull brown plumage, the Spotted Flycatcher's lively flycatching behaviour often draws attention. It is one of the latest summer migrants to reach Britain, arriving during early May, but still quite often manages to produce two broods. It occurs throughout much of Britain in open country with trees and bushes and not infrequently in gardens. Once relatively common, numbers have declined markedly since the 1960s, probably due to difficulties on migration to and from its wintering grounds in southern Africa. It is a very widespread species in Europe.

- **Length** : 13.5–14.5 cm
- **Weight** : 13–20 g
- **Food** : flying insects, some berries
- **Clutch** : 4–5 eggs (May–July)

Pied Flycatcher
Ficedula hypoleuca

A summer migrant to Britain's oak woods, the Pied Flycatcher nests in tree holes. It will readily take to nesting in suitable nest boxes – in some areas nearly the whole population may use them. This makes it a favourite subject for studies of breeding biology. It can be quite easy to find in most suitable woodlands in Wales, western England and south-west Scotland; it is however absent as a breeding species from the rest of England, most of Scotland and all of Ireland. Large numbers of birds from Scandinavia often arrive on the east coast during autumn migration. The female has a light brown and white version of the male's pattern.

- **Length :** 12–13 cm
- **Weight :** 9–17 g
- **Food :** small flying insects, caterpillars
- **Clutch :** 5–7 eggs (May)

Long-tailed Tit
Aegithalos caudatus

Easily identified, social, always on the move and forever calling, it's hard to miss the common and widespread Long-tailed Tit. It occurs throughout the southern half of the British Isles but has a much more patchy distribution in the north and is absent from the western and northern Isles. Pairs nest quite early, hiding their beautiful lichen-covered, feather-stuffed ball of a nest in thick vegetation. Outside the breeding season, family groups roam through woodland, hedgerows, parks and large gardens, feeding acrobatically as they go. These noisy flocks are often followed by other species, usually tits but also the occasional treecreeper or warbler. They are common on much of the continent.

- **Length :** 13.5–14.5 cm
- **Weight :** 6–10 g
- **Food :** small insects, spiders
- **Clutch :** 8–10 eggs (March–June)

Marsh Tit

Parus palustris

Very similar in appearance to the Willow Tit, the Marsh Tit is best identified by its distinctive *pitchou* call. Once quite widespread and relatively common residents of the woodlands of much of southern Britain, both species are declining. The Marsh Tit is absent from many areas in the northern of England, most of Scotland and north-west Wales. It occurs in gardens in rural areas and one or two birds will often come to a favoured feeder. Both species are widespread over the much of Europe (excepting Spain and Portugal), although the Marsh Tit's distribution is generally more southerly.

- **Length :** 11–13 cm
- **Weight :** 9–13 g
- **Food :** inseces, spiders, seeds
- **Clutch :** 4–9 eggs (April–June)

Willow Tit

Parus montanus

Very similar in appearance to the Marsh Tit, it wasn't until 1900 that the Willow Tit was postively identified in Britain, although Willow Tits on the continent are more distinct, being paler and greyer. Hearing the Willow's characteristic nasal *tchay-tchay* call can help in making a definite identification. Its distribution is very similar to that of the Marsh Tit but where both occur it tends to inhabit wetter habitats: riverside woodland, scrub with trees in marshland or near gravel pits. It has declined dramatically in the last 30 years and is generally rarer than the Marsh Tit. It rarely comes to bird tables, and as it excavates its own nest hole it is unlikely to use nest boxes.

- **Length :** 11–13 cm
- **Weight :** 10–13 g
- **Food :** small insects and spiders, some seeds
- **Clutch :** 7–9 eggs (April–June)

Crested Tit

Parus cristatus

- **Length :** 11–12 cm
- **Weight :** 10–12 g
- **Food :** insects, larvae, seeds
- **Clutch :** 5–7 eggs (April–June)

In Britain the perky Crested Tit has a very restricted distribution, living only in natural Caledonian pine forest in the Scottish highlands. Abernethy Forest near Aviemore is a good place to find it. This restricted British range is somewhat surprising given that on the continent it is found in all kinds of woodland, although it is still quite closely associated with conifers and is commonest in upland conifer forest. Like some other tits, it stores food during summer to be eaten later in the winter. On the continent it comes to bird tables in gardens with conifers.

Coal Tit

Parus ater

- **Length :** 10.5–11.5 cm
- **Weight :** 8–16 g
- **Food :** insects, spiders, seeds
- **Clutch :** 8–10 eggs (April–June)

The diminutive Coal Tit is less colourful than the Blue and Great Tits and less inclined to come into parks or gardens, and for these reasons is less familiar than the other two. It is, however, quite a common and widespread bird over much of Britain although it prefers areas of conifer or mixed woodland; there are fewer birds in much of eastern and northern England and the species is absent from the northern and western Isles. Although never numerous at bird tables, and much bullied by larger species, a few birds will visit them, especially in more rural areas, and towards the end of winter when their hidden stores of natural food are running out.

Blue Tit
Parus caeruleus

Along with its larger cousin the Great Tit, the Blue Tit is one of our most familiar birds. It is the classic bird-table visitor and nest-box user, common throughout most of Britain wherever there are trees, bushes or hedgerows. As with the Great Tit the only places where the Blue Tit does not occur in Britain are the northern and western isles of Scotland. It is an intelligent and adaptable bird, which famously learnt to open foil milk bottle tops to take the cream from the top of the milk; a behaviour which must be partly to blame for the decline of the British milkman. Common and widespread over much of Europe, it is in Britain that the Blue Tit is most abundant.

- **Length :** 11–12 cm
- **Weight :** 9–16 g
- **Food :** insects, caterpillars, seeds
- **Clutch :** 9–13 eggs (April–June)

Great Tit
Parus major

The largest of the tit family and one of the most common and widespread, the Great Tit is easily recognised by its white cheeks and black stripe down its yellow belly. Resident, it occurs almost everywhere in Britain where there are some bushes and trees; absent only from the Hebrides, Orkney and Shetland. Very common in gardens and parks, it is one of the most regular visitors to bird tables in winter and will readily occupy man-made structures for nesting, nest boxes and letter boxes are favourites. The characteristic two-note *teacher, teacher* song is often heard, but it also possesses a bewildering array of other calls.

- **Length :** 12–14.5 cm
- **Weight :** 15–22 g
- **Food :** insects, spiders, seeds
- **Clutch :** 7–11 eggs (April–June)

Corsican Nuthatch
Sitta whiteheadi

- **Length** : 12 cm
- **Weight** : 12–14 g
- **Food** : pine seeds, some insects
- **Clutch** : 5–6 eggs (May)

The tiny Corsican Nuthatch has one of the most restricted ranges of any European bird. As its name applies it occurs only on Corsica. Even there it can be difficult to find. It inhabits the high-altitude conifer forests in the centre of the island at an altitude of 700 to 1,200 metres, wherever there are numerous dead trees. The Tartagine forest in the north and Ospedale forest in the south are the best places to look but with a total (world) population of only 2,000 pairs even here they are never numerous. In winter, they move slightly lower and can sometimes be found roaming the forest in company of other birds such as tits.

Nuthatch
Sitta europaea

- **Length** : 13–14.5 cm
- **Weight** : 20–25 g
- **Food** : insects, spiders, seeds
- **Clutch** : 6–8 eggs (March–May)

The agile Nuthatch climbs on tree trunks and branches in search of insects, like a woodpecker, but unlike them it will run head-first down a trunk. It cracks nuts by wedging them in a bark crevice and using its sturdy bill to hammer them open. A common bird in the south of Britain, it is found year-round everywhere there are large trees: in mature forests, parks and large gardens. Further north it becomes quite rare; it is absent from Ireland and most of Scotland. It is a regular visitor to garden bird tables. It nests in tree holes, using mud to narrow the entrance to its preferred dimensions. It is a common resident over much of the continent.

Wallcreeper
Tichodroma muraria

The enigmatic Wallcreeper is a much sought-after and very elusive species. Individuals very occasionally turn up in Britain, causing much excitement when they do. A small bird that spends its life climbing and fluttering along rock faces constantly flicking its wings, at first glance it might be mistaken for a giant moth. It nests very high up in the highest of southern Europe's mountains and, although not rare, it can be very hard to find during the breeding season. In winter it takes up residence on large cliffs or old buildings at much lower altitudes and at this time is easier to see; birds are present in most rocky gorges along the Mediterranean coast, although they can turn up almost anywhere.

- **Length** : 16–17 cm
- **Weight** : 16–22 g
- **Food** : small insects and spiders
- **Clutch** : 3–5 eggs (May–June)

Treecreeper and Short-toed Treecreeper
Certhia familiaris and
Certhia brachydactyla

It's relatively easy to identify a bird as one of the treecreepers, but separating the two is almost impossible in the field. The Short-toed (pictured) is browner underneath but this is hard to see well. They're confiding, unobtrusive little birds that run up tree trunks and along branches searching in the bark for insects with their thin decurved bills. Only the resident Treecreeper occurs in Britain (the Short-toed is an extremely rare vagrant) and is found where there are large trees: woodland, large overgrown hedgerows, parks and well-wooded gardens. The Short-toed Treecreeper is the more familiar species on much of the southern half of Europe, being replaced by the 'British' species in upland areas and more northern countries.

- **Length** : 12–13 cm
- **Weight** : 7–10 g
- **Food** : small insects and spiders
- **Clutch** : 5–6 eggs (April–July)

Golden Oriole
Oriolus oriolus

- **Length :** 22–25 cm
- **Weight :** 70–80 g
- **Food :** insects, spiders, fruit
- **Clutch :** 3–4 eggs (May–July)

Once you have found one, the male Golden Oriole is easily identified. However, the species is very rare in Britain with just a few pairs breeding each year in stands of poplar in East Anglia and some lost migrants at coastal sites. It is quite common and widespread over all but the north of Europe, and is present from April to August. It inhabits warm (often south-facing) open deciduous woodland, usually near water. It can be extremely difficult to see as it nearly always keeps hidden in treetop foliage, although the male's fluty song is distinctive. Females are duller and greener. On the continent they sometimes come to gardens to eat cherries.

Red-backed Shrike
Lanius collurio

- **Length :** 16–18 cm
- **Weight :** 25–40 g
- **Food :** mainly insects, also rodents, frogs
- **Clutch :** 5–6 eggs (May–June)

Once common enough in Britain to have a nickname ('butcherbird' from its habit of impaling excess prey on thorns), the Red-backed Shrike is no longer a breeding bird in Britain, disappearing in the 1980s. Why it became extinct here is not clear but its decline in Britain is part of a wider reduction of its distribution in north-western Europe. Today the only birds that are now seen in Britain are off-course individuals – a few turn up each year during migration. It is still quite common and widespread in the southern half of Europe between May and August when it can be found in many areas with patches of scrub or overgrown hedges, particularly with thorn bushes.

Great Grey Shrike
Lanius excubitor

The largest European shrike is by no means common here, but every year some Scandinavian birds arrive for the winter when they need an extensive area to be able to find enough food. They occupy open areas with scrub and scattered bushes, establishing a territory that they will defend against other individuals of the species. They hunt by looking for prey whilst perched immobile on a prominent open perch; this makes them relatively easy to find. This species breeds and winters over much of the northern two-thirds of Europe, in the south it is replaced by the similar Southern Grey Shrike.

- **Length** : 24–25 cm
- **Weight** : 60–75 g
- **Food** : insects, small rodents, birds
- **Clutch** : 5–6 eggs (April–May)

Southern Grey Shrike
Lanius meridionalis

Once considered a form of the Great Grey Shrike, this southern version is now recognised as a different species. It occurs in the very south of France, much of the Iberian peninsula and North Africa. It can be easily mistaken for the smaller but similarly coloured Lesser Grey Shrike, which is now a very rare breeding species in its restricted range in southern Europe. Like all shrikes it hunts by waiting motionless on a prominent perch, flying down to catch anything considered edible. This species tends to occupy less open, more bushy ground than the other species of shrike.

- **Longueur** : 24-25 cm
- **Weight** : 50–70 g
- **Food** : large insects, lizards
- **Clutch** : 5–6 eggs (April–May)

Woodchat Shrike
Lanius senator

A migrant to the southern half of Europe, only a few Woodchat Shrikes ever reach Britain and these never stay to breed. This smartly patterned and quite confiding bird is usually easy to identify and to observe. It tends to occur in more open country than other shrikes, often in grazed areas with hedgerows and isolated large trees, sometimes near orchids. Although it will perch on wires and the tops of bushes like other shrikes, it also often uses a dead branch halfway up a large tree and can thus be harder to spot than the other species. It is quite common from May to September in southern France, Spain, Portugal, Italy and the Mediterranean islands.

- **Length :** 16–18 cm
- **Weight :** 33–45 g
- **Food :** mainly insects, also rodents, lizards
- **Clutch :** 5–6 eggs (May-June)

Jay
Garrulus glandarius

This familiar species, by far the brightest member of the crow family, inhabits wooded areas and sometimes parks and large gardens, especially those with oaks. It is usually rather shy, and often all that is seen of it is a white rump disappearing through the foliage, perhaps accompanied with a loud, raucous call. It is very dependant on acorns, spending much of its time in the autumn gathering and hoarding them for a winter food supply. A quite widespread species in England, Wales and southern Scotland occurring wherever there's a good number of oak trees, it is quite uncommon in Ireland. It's also a widespread species in most of Europe.

- **Length :** 32–37 cm
- **Weight :** 145–195 g
- **Food :** acorns, seeds, insects
- **Clutch :** 5–6 eggs (April–May)

Magpie
Pica pica

Another striking crow, easily identified by its black-and-white plumage and very long tail, the cheeky and adaptable Magpie is anything but shy. It is common and widespread over the whole of England, Wales and Ireland and is easy to see where it occurs; it is however, surprisingly rare or absent throughout most of Scotland. The nest is placed high in a tree and easily identified, as this is the only species of any size to construct a roof over its stick nest. It is usually seen in pairs during the breeding season, but otherwise tends to gather in small, often quarrelsome, groups. It's also a very common and widespread species on the continent.

- **Length :** 42–50 cm
- **Weight :** 155–255 g
- **Food :** insects, snails, worms, seeds
- **Clutch :** 6–7 eggs (April–July)

Alpine Chough
Pyrrhocorax graculus

The Alpine Chough is not a British bird; anybody wanting to see this charming species will have to travel to the higher mountains of southern Europe. It is a highly gregarious and vocal species – in suitable habitat within the species range it is hard to miss. Large flocks ride the currents along rock faces or come tumbling out of the sky to land and feed for a while on an Alpine meadow or even on waste dropped by tourists at ski resorts. The less numerous Chough may often associate with them; be careful as young Choughs also have yellowish bills. The nearest places to Britain to see the species are the higher areas of the Alps and especially the Pyrenees.

- **Length :** 37–38 cm
- **Weight :** 160–260 g
- **Food :** insects, small animals, wild fruits and berries
- **Clutch :** 3–5 eggs (May)

Chough
Pyrrhocorax pyrrhocorax

This attractive crow's name is derived from its call. It occupies the wild, rugged coastal cliffs of our western seaboard and even here has a very limited distribution. The west and south coasts of Ireland, Islay and the Isle of Man are the only places it can be considered at all common, with smaller numbers along much of the Welsh coast. After an absence of some 50 years a pair (probably originating from France) recently bred in Cornwall and with a little luck and much conservation effort the Chough may now be increasing in Britain. Look for it feeding on well-grazed turf near to the sea.

- **Length** : 35–38 cm
- **Weight** : 300–350 g
- **Food** : insects, spiders, worms, seeds
- **Clutch** : 3–5 eggs (April–May)

Jackdaw
Corvus monedula

The smallest member of the crow family, the Jackdaw is often seen in cheerful noisy flocks flying around church towers, large old buildings or cliff faces. Here it nests in loose colonies using any suitable crevice; other birds breed less noticeably in hollows in woodland and park trees. It feeds on any open land, often in the company of Rooks or other crows. It is resident throughout most of the British Isles and particularly common in Ireland; the far north-west of Scotland is the only area without them. It is widespread and common throughout all but the very north of Europe.

- **Length** : 32–34 cm
- **Weight** : 195–225 g
- **Food** : insects, larvae, grain
- **Clutch** : 3–6 eggs (April–May)

Rook

Corvus frugilegus

The noise and activity of Rooks at a rookery high in the tops of tall trees is a common enough sight throughout much of rural Britain and Europe. This species is very much associated with farmland and is commoner in areas of livestock rearing than on arable land, although flocks are often seen on newly ploughed land. Very similar to the Carrion Crow, adults are relatively easy to separate as they have a patch of bare pale skin between the bill and eye, but in young Rooks this difference isn't present. Rooks are far more sociable than crows. They occur in much of Europe but are absent from the far north and the Mediterranean area.

- **Length :** 43–48 cm
- **Weight :** 400–530 g
- **Food :** vegetable matter, insects, worms
- **Clutch :** 3–5 eggs (March–April)

Carrion Crow

Corvus corone

The all-black Carrion crow and the grey-and-black Hooded crow were until recently considered to be the same species. Though much commoner in Britain, the Carrion Crow has a much more restricted world range than the Hooded, occurring exclusively in western Europe where it is common and widespread. It is found in all kinds of habitat, including city centres where it can be very confiding. Birds are usually seen alone, in pairs or small family groups. They have the habit of perching motionless at the top of a tall tree as they survey the surroundings for food.

- **Length :** 43–49 cm
- **Weight :** 450–600 g
- **Food :** vegetable matter and small animals
- **Clutch :** 4–5 eggs (April–May)

Hooded Crow
Corvus cornix

- **Length :** 43–49 cm
- **Weight :** 450–600 g
- **Food :** vegetable matter and small animals
- **Clutch :** 4–5 eggs (April–May)

This grey-and-black crow has a restricted range in Britain, replacing the Carrion Crow in north-west Scotland and Ireland. Where these two species meet there is an overlap zone and here mixed pairs produce fertile young intermediate in plumage between Carrion and Hooded. In Europe it's the Hooded Crow that predominates with nearly all birds east of a line from Scandinavia to Italy being of this species. Some Scandinavian birds move south for the winter and a few of these birds occur on the east coast of England each winter.

Raven
Corvus frugilegus

- **Length :** 60–67 cm
- **Weight :** 1–1.4 kg
- **Food :** dead animals, insects
- **Clutch :** 4–6 eggs (February–March)

The largest of the crow family, the Raven was once common and widespread throughout Britain; in the 17th century they fought with Red Kites as they scavenged in the streets of London. Long considered a nuisance to game and stock it has been persecuted for a long time and today breeds in wild areas, particularly along inaccessible coasts in south-west England, Wales, western Scotland and most of Ireland. With enlightened times more and more birds are breeding inland but as a carrion feeder it still suffers from pesticides in sheep-dips and may never recolonise the now arable farmland of eastern England. It has a patchy distribution in Europe, tending to occur in remote areas with livestock.

Starling

Sturnus vulgaris

One of Britain's most widespread and common species, the Starling occurs throughout the year and almost everywhere in the British Isles, only very high ground in northern Scotland is without them. It normally nests in tree cavities but seems just as happy to use a nest box and even drystone walls in the treeless Shetlands. It becomes even commoner in winter as many migrants arrive from northern Europe. At this time of year enormous roosting flocks occur in many areas; often in reedbeds or scrub but even in town-centre trees where night temperatures are slightly higher than those in the countryside.

- **Length :** 17–21 cm
- **Weight :** 60–95 g
- **Food :** insects, worms, larvae, fruit
- **Clutch :** 4–6 eggs (March–June)

Spotless Starling

Sturnus unicolor

Not a British bird, this species is very similar indeed to the much more widespread Starling. It is most easily separated during the breeding season, although even then a close look may be necessary. It has a restricted range; resident, it breeds throughout most of the Iberian Peninsula, in Corsica and the very south-west of mainland France, Sardinia and Sicily, and Mediterranean North Africa. It uses very much the same sort of habitat as the Starling, preferring farmland with open woodland and avoiding very dry areas, uplands and conifer plantations. It can be common around villages, often nesting under roof tiles, and will readily take to using nest boxes.

- **Length :** 17–21 cm
- **Weight :** 60–95 g
- **Food :** insects, worms, larvae, fruit
- **Clutch :** 4–6 eggs (March–June)

House Sparrow
Passer domesticus

- **Length :** 13.5–15 cm
- **Weight :** 25–35 g
- **Food :** seeds, fruits, insects
- **Clutch :** 4–6 eggs (April–July)

Who would have thought, just a few years ago, that the birding press would be full of news concerning the drastic reduction in the numbers of the House Sparrow? Once common everywhere, the recent declines of a species that never deserved a second look have brought bird conservation into everyday life. Still resident and widespread in all but the remotest areas of the British Isles, its almost complete disappearance from, for example, the city of London is a cause for concern, especially as no explanation for its decline has been found. It seems to be suffering the same plight over much of continental Europe.

Tree Sparrow
Passer montanus

- **Length :** 14 cm
- **Weight :** 18–26 g
- **Food :** seeds, insects, fruit
- **Clutch :** 4–6 eggs (April–July)

This is a charming little bird that has recently suffered a very severe decline throughout most of Britain. A resident species, it has a very strange distribution, being commoner in the east of England, Scotland and Ireland, the Midlands and much of southern England, but rare or absent from most of the south-west, Wales, and most of Scotland and Ireland. It normally occurs in rural areas wherever there are open spaces and abundant large trees, but not in woodland or highly urbanised areas. Feeding stations, often at nature reserves but also in private gardens, seem to have helped to begin to reverse the decline.

Chaffinch
Fringilla coelebs

The Chaffinch is one of the commonest and most widespread of British birds. It breeds and winters everywhere, except for the highest parts of the Scottish Highlands, the Orkneys, Shetlands and Hebrides. As a breeding species it can be quite secretive although it nests almost anywhere where there are bushes and trees, even in city-centre parks. In winter it becomes even more common with birds coming from the continent, many coming to feed in gardens. It is quite interesting to note that its specific scientific name *coelebs*, given to the species by the famous Swedish naturalist Linnaeus, means 'bachelor'; in Sweden many more of the dull brown females than the colourful males leave for the winter.

- **Length :** 14.5–16 cm
- **Weight :** 17–30 g
- **Food :** seeds, berries, insects
- **Clutch :** 4–5 eggs (April–June)

Brambling
Fringilla montifringilla

The Brambling is a close northern relative of the Chaffinch, and looks superficially similar to that species. It is a winter visitor to Britain, when it comes from northern Europe in search of beechmast, the seeds of the beech tree. As the beech crop varies in quantity from one area to another and from one year to the next, so does the abundance of the Brambling. It occurs throughout Britain but its occurrence is hard to predict. When natural food is short at the end of winter, look for the occasional bird in the garden feeding with the Chaffinches. It breeds commonly in Scandinavia, and very occasionally in Scotland.

- **Length :** 14–16 cm
- **Weight :** 20–34 g
- **Food :** seeds, (especially beechmast and maize), insects
- **Clutch :** 6–7 eggs (May–July)

Serin

Serinus serinus

- **Length :** 11–12 cm
- **Weight :** 10–14 g
- **Food :** seeds, buds, some insects
- **Clutch :** 4 eggs (March–August)

Avery rare species in Britain, it was once thought that this lively little finch might colonise the south-east of England but it has yet to do so with just a handful of breeding records. This is rather surprising as it is quite a common breeding bird of parks and large gardens in many rural areas of southern Europe as far north as Belgium, Holland and much of Germany; these birds move south-west for the winter to join others of the species around the Mediterranean and in much of Spain and Portugal. It is easiest to locate in the spring when the male gives its characteristic rapid jingling song from an exposed perch.

Greenfinch

Carduelis chloris

- **Length :** 13–15 cm
- **Weight :** 25–35 g
- **Food :** seeds, buds, insects
- **Clutch :** 4–5 eggs (April–August)

Avery common and widespread species, this large greenish finch is now familiar to many people as one of the most frequent visitors to bird feeders. A resident species in Britain, it breeds throughout the country, only avoiding parts of the far north and upland areas. Once considered a bird of arable land, it is increasingly turning to urban areas as its main food, seeds, have become harder to find on farmland due to increased use of herbicides. Its winter distribution is very similar, with a little movement by some birds to lower ground. Common over most of Europe.

Goldfinch
Carduelis carduelis

The Goldfinch is an inhabitant of cultivated areas with bushes and hedgerows, of scrub and also large, well-wooded parks and gardens; common throughout Britain except in the far north, western islands and open upland areas. The colourful adults (male and female are very similar) are easy to identify; young birds don't have the adult's characteristic red face but do have the yellow wing-bars. It has a longish pointed bill used for extracting small seeds from wild plants, especially thistles and their relatives. It can also be attracted to gardens by cultivating suitable plants and letting them seed or by feeding nyjer seed (advertised as the 'Goldfinch magnet').

- **Length :** 11.5–12.5 cm
- **Weight :** 13–19 g
- **Food :** small seeds, insects
- **Clutch :** 5 eggs (March–July)

Siskin
Carduelis spinus

This handsome little finch is becoming easier to see in the British Isles. It tends to breed in mature conifer forests and has increased with the increase in the area of Britain's mature conifer forests. During the breeding season it is commonest in the west and north, with outlying populations in the south in such places as the New Forest. It is more widespread in winter and may turn up wherever there are fruiting alders. Since the 1960s, it has also taken to visiting many gardens to feed on peanuts. Winter numbers are increased by birds arriving from the continent where it is quite widespread, especially in northern countries.

- **Length :** 11–12.5 cm
- **Weight :** 12–14 g
- **Food :** seeds, berries, insects
- **Clutch :** 3–5 eggs (March–July)

Linnet
Carduelis cannabina

- **Length :** 13–14 cm
- **Weight :** 16–21 g
- **Food :** seeds, a few insects
- **Clutch :** 4–6 eggs (March–August)

With its bright pink breast and forehead the male is relatively easy to identify, the less distinctive, mainly brown and grey females and young can be much harder. This delightful little finch can be found throughout much of Britain, especially in areas of heath where gorse is abundant and along the coast; it also inhabits scrub and overgrown hedgerows. It is absent from much of northern Scotland and upland areas of England where to some extent it is replaced by the similar Twite. A resident, it forms flocks with other finch species outside the breeding season but unlike most hardly ever comes to gardens for food.

Crossbill
Loxia curvirostra

- **Length :** 16–17 cm
- **Weight :** 26–44 g
- **Food :** conifer seeds
- **Clutch :** 3–4 eggs (January–May)

A species of conifer forests (especially where spruce trees are common), the Crossbill feeds almost exclusively on conifer seeds, extracting them from cones using its peculiar cross-tipped bill. A very localised species in Britain, it is usually difficult to find as it nearly always feeds high in the tops of mature trees and changes breeding sites regularly. Numbers varying greatly according to food availability, there are occasional very good years following a large cone crop, when birds from the continent invade Britain. The almost identical Scottish Crossbill is the only species of bird found nowhere but Britain. It is found in the Scottish Highlands; an area that also has good numbers of the 'ordinary' Crossbill. In both species males are brick-red while females are dull green.

Bullfinch

Pyrrhula pyrrhula

With a subdued song and retiring habits, the relatively common and widely distributed Bullfinch is never easy to see, despite the male's bright colours. It occurs throughout most of Britain and Ireland, wherever there are areas with large hedgerows, well-wooded parks, extensive scrub or open woodland, orchards (where it can cause damage by eating the buds of fruit trees) and large gardens. It is absent from upland areas and much of the far north. It usually occurs in pairs or small family groups, which give their presence away with distinctive soft contact calls. Common over much of Europe, especially in areas with conifers, it retains its shy, retiring habits everywhere. Females (photo) have a subdued version of the males' colour pattern.

- **Length** : 14–18 cm
- **Weight** : 18–36 g
- **Food** : seeds, buds, and some insects
- **Clutch** : 4–5 eggs (April–July)

Hawfinch

Coccothraustes coccothraustes

The largest of our finches, this is also probably the most difficult to find although, once found, it is easily identified. It has a restricted range over Britain, occupying large tracts of mixed broadleaved woodland or extensive mature orchards. Quite widespread in the south-east, elsewhere it occurs in a few suitable areas in England, Wales and the south of Scotland. In Britain its habit of lurking quietly in treetops makes it especially difficult to see. Quite common in parts of temperate continental Europe with suitable habitat, small numbers are a regular sight at bird tables, when it often associates with Greenfinches.

- **Length** : 16–17 cm
- **Weight** : 54–56 g
- **Food** : hard seeds, buds
- **Clutch** : 5 eggs (March–June)

Yellowhammer
Emberiza citrinella

- **Length :** 16–17 cm
- **Weight :** 20–35 g
- **Food :** insects, spiders, seeds (winter)
- **Clutch :** 3–4 eggs (April–August)

A resident and probably the most widespread and commonest bunting in Britain, the Yellowhammer used to occur throughout lowland agricultural Britain. Like many other common farmland species its numbers are decreasing and it is now absent from much of the far north and west and a great deal of Ireland, especially where livestock rearing is the principal agricultural activity. However, on much of the arable land of the south and east and the Midlands its *little-bit-of-bread-and-no-cheese* song is still a common sound from the top of a hedgerow bush or tree during much of the spring and summer. Females are much duller though they do have a slight yellow tinge.

Cirl Bunting
Emberiza cirlus

- **Length :** 15–16 cm
- **Weight :** 17–25 g
- **Food :** insects, seeds (winter)
- **Clutch :** 3–4 eggs (May–August)

The confiding Cirl Bunting has a very restricted range in the British Isles after severe declines – it now only breeds in southern Devon. There has been much recent conservation work designed to help the species which appears to be working well; including a joint program of releasing birds into former haunts in Cornwall. It is a widespread and common species throughout much of the south of Europe, especially around the Mediterranean; males give their simple cheerful song from a high perch throughout much of the year in large gardens, parks, overgrown hedgerows and open scrub. Females are dull streaky brown, very like female Yellowhammers.

Rock Bunting
Emberiza cia

The unobtrusive Rock Bunting is a species of the southern half of Europe, not occuring in Britain. Most birds breed at altitude, just above the tree line, where they frequent dry, open, rocky areas with scattered bushes. Although not a migrant it tends to move to lower altitudes for the winter when it uses the same sort of habitat, which can include vineyards and garrigue. In very hard winters they can be found in unusual sites, even visiting gardens. Not rare, but seldom easy to find, on the continent it can be found in many suitable areas of the Alps, Pyrenees, in the Massif Central and throughout much of Spain, Italy and Greece.

- **Length** : 15–16.5 cm
- **Weight** : 19–21 g
- **Food** : seeds, insects, larvae
- **Clutch** : 4 eggs (May–July)

Ortolan Bunting
Emberiza hortulana

This migrant bunting is a very rare visitor to Britain and is declining over much of western Europe. This decline may well be due to its having been heavily hunted in parts of southern Europe (including south-west France) in the past, where it was considered a delicacy. Now protected, the species' continuing bad fortunes can be blamed (as with so many other species) on habitat destruction through agricultural intensification. It is present in France, Spain, Portugal and Italy from April to October, migrating to pass the winter in sub-Saharan Africa. During the breeding season it tends to inhabit dry open areas such as rocky hillsides or vineyards.

- **Length** : 14–16.5 cm
- **Weight** : 19–27 g
- **Food** : insects, larvae, seeds
- **Clutch** : 4–5 eggs (May–July)

Reed Bunting
Emberiza schoeniclus

- **Length :** 13–16 cm
- **Weight :** 13–23 g
- **Food :** seeds, insects, other invertebrates
- **Clutch :** 4–5 eggs (April–July)

As its name suggest, the Reed Bunting tends to inhabit wet areas, usually with reeds, sedges or bulrushes and often with scattered willows that are used as perches. In the breeding plumage the male has a characteristic black head with white collar, otherwise it's quite plain, like the female and young. It is quite a widespread species, nesting in most areas with wetlands but less commonly on higher ground. The winter distribution is very similar with numbers increased by some migrants from the near continent. In most areas a trip to a well-vegetated gravel pit, reservoir or river should provide sightings of the species.

Corn Bunting
Emberiza calandra

- **Length :** 17–18.5 cm
- **Weight :** 42–64 g
- **Food :** especially seeds, some insects
- **Clutch :** 4–5 eggs (April–July)

A rather plain-faced and dull-plumaged bird, the Corn Bunting is nevertheless quite distinctive with its chunky, big-headed and heavy-billed outline. The 'jangling keys' song of the male, typically delivered from an exposed perch in farmland, is becoming a less and less familiar sound as its range retracts. It is found throughout the year on the open arable spaces of the south and east of England and east of Scotland, with isolated populations in such places as the Hebrides, the west coast of Ireland and East Anglian coast; it is absent from much of western Britain. It is common on parts of the southern two-thirds of Europe.

Appendices

Observering birds

Watching birds is becoming a more and more popular pastime. By respecting a few simple rules and with modest financial outlay, you can enjoy rewarding birdwatching whether you live in the town or the countryside.

THE INDISPENSABLE BINOCULARS

Anyone who looks at birds, even occasionally, usually ends up wanting to take a better look, as it's difficult to get close enough to many wild birds without disturbing them. Also, it's only when the observer is at a distance that a bird can be watched behaving naturally. The answer is to invest in a pair of binoculars, the most vital piece of kit for any birdwatcher.

Which binoculars to choose?

Binoculars can be divided into two types that differ in the make-up of their optical system. Porro-prisms have the eye-pieces closer together than the large lenses, while roof-prism binoculars have the eye-pieces and large lenses in line, generally making them less bulky. Porros often give a slightly brighter image.

A binocular's optical powers are denoted by two numbers. The first corresponds to the magnification and the second the diameter of the objective (large) lens in millimetres. So 10 x 42 binoculars magnify the image 10 times, and their objective lens has a diameter of 42 mm. In general, the higher the magnification of a pair of binoculars the bigger and heavier they are, and the less stable the image. Likewise, the larger the coefficient between the two figures the brighter the images seen through the binoculars. So 10 x 42 binoculars have a coefficient of 4.2 (42/10), which is slightly brighter than 8 x 32 (coefficient of 4), but far less so than a 8 x 42 – (coefficient of 5.25).

What to choose

Binoculars exist in all sorts of shapes and sizes with prices varying between £15 and £1,000. So, what to buy?

A pair of good binoculars and comfortable clothing: indispensable for enjoyable birdwatching no matter at what level.

Firstly it's worth bearing in mind that an 8x–10x range of magnification is ideal for birdwatching. Above that (12x, 16x or even 20x) the magnification is too great; finding the bird with the binoculars can be difficult and the image is not stable enough to easily see the bird. Thus, 8 x 32, 8 x 42, 10 x 40 or 10 x 42 are the best for birdwatching.

Porro-prism binoculars are the cheaper option, but are more fragile and generally their optics aren't so good. The lowest priced models (between £15 and £30) can only be for very occasional use. They are certainly not recommended for regular or intensive use as they may well be tiring for the eyes and cause a headache. However, there are porro prism binoculars on the market at £35 to £60 that are of reasonable quality and can be recommended for beginners. Above this price the better porro prism models are stronger with good optics and compare favourably with the lower-priced roof-prism binoculars.

For anyone thinking of birdwatching seriously, roof-prism binoculars have many advantages over porro-prisms: they are compact, have internal focusing which means they are water- and dust-tight, and usually contain a better quality glass in their lenses and prisms. Once again there is a large range in prices, although they are generally more expensive than porro-prism models. There are compact models that cost between £100 and £200, which not only have good optics but have the added advantage of being small and light (they easily fit in a pocket). Their disadvantage is a lack of luminosity which makes them difficult to use in poor light conditions. Between £200 and £600 there are various models made by the best-known names such as Swarovski, Leica, Bushnell, Minolta and Nikon, which suit even the most experienced birdwatcher. However, for the professional or ardent amateur wanting the very best, the top-end roof-prism binoculars are completely water- and dust-proof, are lightweight yet optically close to perfect and are guaranteed for at least 30 years. Most such models are made by Swarovski and Leica, with prices reaching £1,000 or more.

IN SUMMARY:
• for occasional use, good entry-level porro-prism or roof-prism 8 x 30 or 8 x 32 compact binoculars should cost about £40;
• for regular use choose a good quality 8 x 42 or 10 x 42 binocular of either type, price £70 or more;
• for anyone who has caught the bug it is well worth investing in a good pair of roof-prism binoculars (8 x 32 or 10 x 42) for around £200 to £600.
• for those who want the very best, top-end roof-prisms from Leica or Swarovski can cost upwards of £1,000

Adjusting binoculars correctly

Many people don't take the time to adjust their binoculars properly for their own eyesight, and then complain that they're difficult to use. Correct adjustment before use is essential.

In order to see correctly through binoculars it is very important to have the lenses in line with your eyes. If the eye-pieces are too far apart, then a dark area appears in the centre of the image, if they are too close together the dark area appears at the edges of the image. Don't hesitate to change the width between eye-pieces in borrowed binoculars, it can easily be changed again for the owner.

All binoculars have a means of dioptric correction, in case the user has better vision in one eye than the other. Adjustment is easy and only needs to be done once for each user. It is done in three stages;

1. Shut the right eye and focus on a stationary object in the middle distance with the use of the focus wheel.

2. Now shut the left eye and open the right one. If the image isn't clear after a moment then put it into focus using the adjustment around the right-hand eye-piece (or on the central axis in roof-prism models).

3. Now look at the object with both eyes; the image should be perfect, if not repeat the steps above.

Once this pre-focusing has been accomplished, normal focusing is done using the central focusing wheel only. Always focus correctly for a good image and comfortable watching.

OTHER USEFUL EQUIPMENT

A pair of binoculars is the basic tool for birdwatching, but other equipment comes in very useful.

Clothing

It's of little use wearing camouflage gear! Contrary to popular opinion it isn't at all necessary to be dressed like a soldier or a hunter to get close to birds. Of course, if walking in forest, it can be useful to wear dull, rather than brightly coloured clothes but what counts above all is comfort. It's very important to be at ease in your clothing, to be able to move easily and not to be too hot or too cold. Birds have such keen sight and are so sensitive to movement that it's very difficult not to be seen, even if you're disguised as a bush! Better to count on being discreet, silent and calm when getting closer. Pay particular attention to choice of footwear; wellingtons are useful in wet areas and hiking boots on long walks or rocky terrain. When choosing a jacket for birdwatching, pick one that has pockets for essential bits and bobs, is warm and windproof, and doesn't swish or rustle loudly when you move.

A telescope allows the observer to watch birds a long way off, without disturbing them. They are expensive and should be used as an optional addition to good binoculars, not an alternative.

Notebook

As with a personal diary, a birdwatcher's notebook is full of memories of outings: a list of species seen, the day's weather, information on the visited site (name, access, best time for good lighting), notes on the birds' behaviour and the plumages of any unidentified species. It's very important to have a field notebook and pencil when out in the field. Take time out once in a while to note down what you have seen or heard; notes made on the spot are so much more likely to be accurate than those written from memory after the event.

Identification guide

Without a field guide it is impossible to put a name to an unfamiliar bird. Your guide should carried on every outing into the field as it's much easier to identify a bird that's in view, or that's just flown off, than to do so hours afterwards. Looking through an identification guide will also help you learn what to look for. Memorising shapes, colours, names and the illustrations in the book will help in identifying a bird in the field. There are numerous guides to the birds of Britain and Europe which can be used in conjunction with this book (see Recommended reading, page 218).

A CODE OF CONDUCT
Birdwatchers should abide by some simple rules. In doing so there's more chance of more enjoyable observations

Be unobtrusive

The best way of finding birds is by searching for them as a predator does. To do this it's necessary to move slowly, without making sudden movements and keeping quiet (keep your voice low if you have to speak, and tread softly). Keep your eyes open all the time, and your ears too – in woodland most birds are most easily located by their calls. With this approach you also have a better chance of seeing other wild animals such as deer, badgers or foxes. In the countryside it's better to walk along a woodland edge or hedgerow rather than the middle of a field and to walk in the shade rather than in full sun, in order to blend in with the background. Cautious and unselfish behaviour will be appreciated by other countryside users too.

Keep your distance

It's always best to keep a certain distance away from a bird in order not to disturb it or cause it to fly away. When watching from a distance, you may find that the bird comes steadily nearer, sometimes very close; in such cases it's obviously necessary to stay still.

Binoculars should be raised slowly and any movements kept slow. Always bear in mind that, when observing birds for pleasure, the bird's needs must come first. Observing a bird for a while and leaving without having disturbed it is much more rewarding than startling one into flight and watching it quickly disappear, never to be seen again.

Curb your enthusiasm

Without doubt this is one of the most difficult rules to respect. Often, when a bird is first seen (especially if having searched long and hard for it) it is easy to react overexcitedly and scare it away. For example, we might try to indicate a bird's position to others, perhaps by shouting or waving our arms, and the bird is gone before anyone has seen it well. Or we might move too quickly in order to get a better look (rather than waiting for it to move into view) and off it flies. It is sometimes difficult to stay calm, but keeping one's cool can mean better sightings for everyone, and a less frightened bird.

Be patient

Patience is a required quality of a good birdwatcher. Finding a bird can take a long time, seeing it well even longer. Initially birdwatching can be a source of frustration and decep-tion as you might find it hard to see any birds at all, and those you do see may be viewable only under poor conditions. As with many things experience is needed and can be a long time coming. There is, of course, only one remedy – spend as much time as possible looking at birds, and look at them all!

Pick the right places

Although birds may be seen everywhere and anywhere, the occurrence of any given species is seldom a chance affair. Most species occupy a definite habitat outside of which they are rarely seen. It's therefore necessary to know which habitat is preferred by the bird or birds you want to see.

Exploring your local area will soon reveal to you which habitat types are most productive for birds. In general wetlands, forest edges and open spaces with copses are all very good. High ground can be excellent for watching passing migrant birds in spring and autumn, while almost anywhere along the coast has potential; not only for seabirds and shore birds but for migrating birds of all kinds.

It's also important to locate the best spots within any given habitat for seeing birds. Look at every feature in the landscape, whether it be a pylon, electricity cables, a fence post, a dead branch, a farm building, isolated bushes or trees, a herd of livestock, a hedge or the side of a stream or river. If you are looking for birds on open water, take your time and scan the surface several times as many diving species can stay submerged for long spells. Don't forget to check the sky too, many species spend a lot of time on the wing, especially birds of prey.

Time of year is important too. The best time to look for woodland birds is often early spring, when the leaves have not yet come out but the birds have started to sing. Waterbirds are often more numerous in winter, while autumn is best for seeing migrating birds.

Look for vertical elements within the landscape such as hedgerows, posts, isolated trees or even bales of straw, all of which serve as perches. Here the large cliff-face in the distance looks interesting and could well repay a visit.

The colours of birds

In many cases accurately noting a bird's colours will help you identify its species. It is therefore necessary to describe the colour clearly and to try to avoid general terms such as 'dark' or 'light'. A bird that's described as 'dark above and light below' could be black and white or brown and yellow. For the colours that are common in birds' plumages (red, yellow, green, brown, grey) try to define the particular shade or shades. The following examples show different shades of these colours and suggest appropriate names for them. Be careful when describing a colour, as our perception of shade depends on the light conditions at the time and the state of the plumage, for example newly grown feathers may look brighter than old ones, wet plumage usually looks darker than dry feathers, and a bird seen with the light behind it looks far less colourful than when seen in good light.

VARIATIONS OF RED

Red, or more exactly shades of red, are very common in birds' plumage. Here are a few illustrated examples.

Crimson as on the forehead and breast of a male Linnet

Vermillion as on a Goldfinch's face

Pink like the legs and bill of a Greater Flamingo

Salmon-pink like the wash on the male Whitethroat's breast

Chestnut as on the crown of a female Blackcap

Orange like the Kingfisher's breast

Red-brown like the breast band of the Shelduck

VARIATIONS OF YELLOW

**Many birds have some shade of yellow in their plumage, from vivid pure yellow
to soft ochres and creams.**

Bright yellow of the
male Golden Oriole

Lemon like the under-
parts of the Blue Tit

Cream like the
Coal Tit's belly

Fawn of the Collared Dove

Ochre-yellow is an exact
description of the colour
of the Hawfinch's belly

Flesh coloured like the legs of
the Crested Lark and those of
many other birds

VARIATIONS OF GREEN

**Very few birds have bright green in their plumage,
but many have shades of green.**

Olive like the back of
the Yellow Wagtail

Bottle green as the head
of the male Mallard

Khaki like the top of the
male Cirl Bunting's head

Yellow-green as the general
overall colour of the Greenfinch

Grey-green as in the dull
plumage of a Chiffchaff

GREY TONES

Many birds have grey in their plumage and there are all kinds of different shades, these can vary in appearance according to the light.

Mouse-grey like a male Wheatear's back

Silver-grey like a Herring Gull's back

Blue-grey like the plumage of a wild Rock Dove

Brown-grey as the back of a Blackcap

Ash grey like the Crane's plumage

Slate-grey like the colour of the back of a Lesser Black-backed Gull

BROWN TONES

In northern latitudes where unlike the tropics brightly coloured species are the exception, there are many different shades of brown.

Fawn like the Skylark's autumn plumage

Natural brown as in the Robin's plumage

Chestnut like the back of the Fieldfare

Cinnamon-brown like the colour of a Tree Sparrow's crown

Milk-coffee coloured as with Marsh Tit's back

Beige like the Jay's body plumage

Bird classification

Most bird guides use a scientific classification or systematic order to determine the sequence in which they discuss and describe the different bird species. In this system birds are grouped by family (the family name ends with the suffix -idae), and families are grouped into orders (with the suffix –iformes).

These families are arranged in taxonomic order, which reflects the sequence in which the birds are thought to have evolved, the most primitive coming first. It is a good idea to try to learn the basics of this sequence, as it will help you understand more about identification.

The list below shows all the bird orders and families found within the region covered by this book, with examples of the groups or species of birds they contain.

The taxonomic order of families most widely used at the present is that proposed in 1970 by the Dutch taxonomist K.H.Voous, although it has since undergone a few modifications taken into account here.

Anseriformes
Anatidae (swans, geese, ducks)

Galliformes
Tetraonidae (Capercaillie, grouse)
Phasianidae (quail, pheasants, partridges)

Gaviiformes
Gaviidae (divers)

Podicipediformes
Podicipedidae (grebes)

Procellariiformes
Procellariidae (petrels, shearwaters)
Hydrobatidae (storm-petrels)

Pelecaniformes
Sulidae (gannets)
Phalacrocoracidae (cormorants)
Ardeidae (herons, egrets, bitterns)

Ciconiidae (storks)
Threskiornithidae (ibises)

Phoenicopteriformes
Phoenicopteridae (flamingos)

Accipitriformes
Accipitridae (kites, buzzards, eagles, vultures, harriers, hawks)
Pandionidae (Osprey)

Falconiformes
Falconidae (falcons)

Gruiformes
Rallidae (rails, crakes, Moorhen, coots)
Gruidae (cranes)
Otididae (bustards)

Charadriiformes
Haematopodidae (oystercatchers)

Recurvirostridae (avocets and stilts)
Burhinidae (stone-curlews)
Glareolidae (pratincoles)
Charadriidae (plovers)
Scolopacidae (sandpipers, curlews and
 snipe)
Stercorariidae (skuas)
Laridae (gulls)
Sternidae (terns)
Alcidae (auks)

Pteroclidiformes
Pteroclididae (sandgrouse)

Columbiformes
Columbidae (pigeons, doves)

Cuculiformes
Cuculidae (cuckoos)

Strigiformes
Tytonidae (barn owls)
Strigidae (owls)

Caprimulgiformes
Caprimulgidae (nightjars)

Apodiformes
Apodidae (swifts)

Coraciiformes
Alcedinidae (kingfishers)

Meropidae (bee-eaters)
Coraciidae (rollers)
Upupidae (Hoopoe)

Piciformes
Picidae (woodpeckers)

Passeriformes
Alaudidae (larks)
Hirundinidae (swallows, martins)
Motacillidae (pipits, wagtails)
Cinclidae (dippers)
Troglodytidae (Wren)
Prunellidae (accentors)
Turdidae (thrushes)
Sylviidae (warblers, crests)
Muscicapidae (flycatchers, chats, robins)
Timaliidae (babblers, e.g. Bearded Tit
Aegithalidae (long-tailed tits)
Paridae (tits)
Sittidae (nuthatches)
Tichodromadidae (Wallcreeper)
Certhiidae (treecreepers)
Remizidae (penduline tits)
Oriolidae (orioles)
Laniidae (shrikes)
Corvidae (crows)
Sturnidae (starlings)
Passeridae (sparrows)
Fringillidae (finches)
Emberizidae (buntings)

English and scientific names

In the middle of the 18th century, the now famous Swedish naturalist Carl von Linné invented a system for naming all species of animal and plant. Each living organism was given a scientific name formed of two words (usually derived from Latin): the first describing the genus (with a capital letter), the second the species. For example: *Parus* is the genus name for tits, this coupled with the specific name *major* is the scientific name for the Great Tit. These names have the advantage over English names of being universal. So for a French ornithologist the Great Tit is 'Mésange charbonnière' but it is also *Parus major*, and this name identifies it in any language. Scientific names do change occasionally, but only in response to new advances in our understanding of how birds are related to each other. For example, the Little Tern used to have the scientific name *Sterna albifrons*, but it is now known as *Sternula albifrons*, as it was found to be less closely related to the other terns in the genus *Sterna* than was previously thought. Scientific names are usually derived from Latin or Ancient Greek but may also honour a species' discoverer, as in Sabine's Gull *Larus sabini*. Although they are similarly derived, the names of families and orders are not italicised.

Helping birds

Although birds are quite able to survive without man's intervention, we can make their lives easier: by helping them to get through the winter, and by providing them with safe nesting sites.

FEEDING AND ATTRACTING BIRDS

Many people regularly throw out a few scraps for the birds, perhaps a handful of breadcrumbs for the sparrows. By attracting birds close to the house, even to the windowsill, this feeding of garden birds allows us to see them better. Feeding attracts more birds in winter when they're more gregarious and travel more than in spring and summer.

Winter menu

A bird's winter menu has three important components: seeds, fat and fruits. It's also helpful to provide water. It's better to avoid giving salty food, too much dried bread (crumbs only) and dehydrated coconut which may cause digestive disorders; on the other hand leftovers such as steamed vegetables, pasta or rice can be given.

Sunflower seeds are easily the food most appreciated by small birds like tits and finches as they are easily opened (or you can buy them already shelled) and are very calorie-rich. Goldfinches can be attracted by putting out nyjer seed; these very small seeds need a special feeder. Maize and wheat are too tough for most small birds and should be avoided. If buying 'wild bird food' use a reputable make as often these mixes have a high content of seeds that go uneaten.

Unsalted **vegetable fat**, such as margarine, should be used in preference to animal fat as it contains fewer toxins. Nevertheless, suet or lard are good substitutes; suet can be melted, mixed with sunflower seeds and then allowed to set to form a 'bird cake much appreciated by tits, nuthatches and woodpeckers.

A mix of fat and sunflower seeds is much appreciated by Blue Tits.

Fruit, even partly rotten, can be put out for Blackbirds and other thrushes; it will also be appreciated by starlings, Robins and sparrows. Apples are often used as they keep well over the winter, but any uncooked fruit can be used.

With these basic foods it's also necessary to provide **water**, often inaccessible during freezing conditions or periods with snow in winter. Use a shallow, flat receptacle and fill it with water regularly at the same time each day. If it's very cold and the water freezes quickly it's enough to refill the receptacle from time to time (at least once in the morning and once in the evening so that the birds become accustomed to the times). There's no point in using hot water as it freezes just as quickly. Use plain tap water with nothing added.

Siting a bird table

Whether the food is served on a fantastic bird table in the shape of an alpine chalet or simply placed on a plate on the windowsill or the ground outside makes little difference to the birds. Nowadays it's possible to buy all sorts of bird tables from specialist shops or conservation organisations, or to make one oneself; in all cases, it's important to respect a few simple rules as far as possible.

The security of birds that have been attracted must be a priority. It's inevitable that a concentration of many small birds will attract predators, especially cats. Thus it's far better to place the bird feeder at a certain height (on its own pole is the best solution) and with good all-round visibility so the birds can see danger approaching. Nearby cover could conceal a hunting cat but equally offers an escape for small birds should a Sparrowhawk attempt to catch them, so a compromise is best.

Hygiene shouldn't be forgotten, either. Dropped food, together with bird droppings, is a haven for bacteria such as salmonella. The fact that many birds are visiting the same spot means diseases could quickly spread. It is therefore essential to clean any feeder regularly and empty them of debris daily. It's a good idea to clean feeders with soapy water once a week or so. There is less waste if food is put out in the early morning; in any case avoid putting out fresh food in the late afternoon, especially on the table or on the ground. Lots of uneaten food left out overnight could attract rats.

Finally, once feeding has stopped (or slowed down) in the spring give the feeders a good clean-out with diluted bleach; rinse and dry them thoroughly before refilling.

A home for birds

Certain birds such as tits and sparrows construct their nests in cavities: a hollow tree, hole in a wall, even in a letterbox. However, in a world that's always becoming more neat and tidy it can be hard to find the perfect site. Luckily many species of bird happily take to wooden nest boxes, built and sited specially for them. Most garden nest boxes are used by Great and Blue Tits but other species can be enticed to nest too.

CHOICE OF NEST BOX
Ready-made nest boxes

As with bird tables there's a large choice of ready-made nest boxes at various outlets. However, beware, many aren't particularly suitable for birds and some can be a real danger for the young inside.

Many are too small, not deep enough and have insufficient space inside, putting chicks at risk of chilling in heavy rain or suffocating in very hot weather. A shallow nest box and too-large entrance hole also allows a cat to reach the nestlings at the bottom. Therefore, choose a nest box with internal dimensions of at least 13 x 13 cm and an access hole at least 15 cm above the inside of the floor. To be on the safe side it is probably best to buy nest boxes from conservation organisations whose designs will have the needs of the bird in mind rather than aesthetic sensibilities. These organisations may also offer specialised nest boxes for other species, such as House Martins, Swifts and owls.

The size of the **access hole** determines which species will use the box. The Blue Tit needs an entrance hole 25 to 28 mm wide, which will exclude a Great Tit, its main competitor. The Great prefers an entrance hole 28 to 34 mm wide. A 45 mm hole (in a correspondingly larger box) will suit Starlings. Many nest boxes sold in general outlets have a perch in front of the entrance hole. This is unnecessary, and also allows predators (including cats) easier access to the chicks. It's better

to avoid such a box, or to saw off the perch.

The choice of **construction material** can also be important as it affects the strength and life of the box. Many are made of light plywood and don't last very long. Those made of planks (at least 15 mm thick) or woodcrete (concrete/sawdust mix) or other resistant materials are better. Plastic and clay boxes should be avoided.

Homemade nest boxes

It's relatively easy to make a very good nest box oneself; use rough unplaned wood without any treatment, according to the following dimensions:

• for **Blue Tits**: make a box with a base at least 13 x 13 cm in the interior and height of at least 23 cm.; the round entrance hole (cut with a special bit or with electric saw and then smoothed with a file – the hole needn't be perfect) should be at least 15 cm above the floor and have a diameter of 25-29 mm:

• for **Great Tits** : the floor should measure at least 14 x 14 cm and the box at least 25 cm in height; the entrance hole should be at least 20 cm above the floor of the box with an entrance hole of 28–34 mm diameter.

In all cases make sure that the roof covers the whole box, with a small overhang at the front so that rain doesn't go near the entrance hole. A piece of wood (approximately 30 x 4 x 2 cm) screwed to the back of the box will allow you to easily attach it to a tree or wall. A few small holes drilled into the bottom of the box will provide a little ventilation and a drier interior. The box will last longer if screws, rather than nails, are used.

Placing the nest box in the garden

The siting of the nest box is very important and greatly influences the occupant's chances of success. Whatever type of nest box is used it should be placed in a quiet, inaccessible and shady spot.

A tree trunk is often the best support. Here suspend the box with its back to the trunk, using electrical wire (strong, supple and hard-wearing) wrapped around the base of a large branch. This will prevent the nest box slipping downwards. The garage wall, house gable, even a large post are all acceptable if there's no suitable tree. The way the box is fixed obviously depends on the support you are using.

Follow some simple rules...

The nest box should be placed at least 2–3 metres above the ground; it can be more. Orientation isn't important but should be done in a way that avoids exposure to rain and the dominant wind. The entrance hole should look out on an open space, of grass if possible.

To ensure that a wooden nest box is safe for nesting birds, make sure it is securely attached and give it a general inspection and a clean-out each autumn.

To find out more...

As your interest in wild birds grows, you will want to learn more about them. Here is a selection of useful reading material, and a list of European bird conservation societies.

RECOMMENDED READING

RSPB Pocket Guide to British Birds by Simon Harrap. A compact, informative and beautifully illustrated guide to 170 of the most common birds found in Britain.

RSPB My First Book of Garden Birds by Mike Unwin and Sarah Whittley. A very attractive book that will help young children (4–8 year olds) discover and identify the most common birds, and to learn more about their lives.

RSPB Children's Guide to Birdwatching by David Chandler and Mike Unwin. An informative and lively guide for 8–12 year olds that will greatly enhance their enjoyment of birdwatching and help to engender a lifetime of enthusiasm for birds and birding.

Collins Bird Guide by Lars Svensson, Killian Mullarney, Dan Zetterström and Peter Grant. The most modern and complete general field guide to all the species of Europe. The illustrations and text are excellent.

Where to Watch Birds in Britain by Simon Harrap and Nigel Redman. A comprehensive guide to the best birdwatching sites throughout Britain, with full access details and many maps.

Secret Lives of British Birds and *Secret Lives of Garden Birds*, by Dominic Couzens with illustrations by Peter Partington. Both books take an in-depth look at the extraordinary hidden lives of some of our most familiar, and some not so familiar, birds.

ORGANISATIONS

Royal Society for the Protection of Birds (RSPB)
The Lodge
Sandy
Bedfordshire
SG19 2DL
tel: (01767) 680551
fax: (01767) 692365
website: www.rspb.org.uk

BirdLife International
Wellbrook Court
Girton Road
Cambridge CB3 0NA
tel: (01223) 277318
fax: (01223) 277200
email: birdlife@birdlife.org
website: www.birdlife.org

British Trust for Ornithology (BTO)
The Nunnery
Thetford
Norfolk IP24 2PU
tel: (01842) 750050
fax: (01842) 750030
email: btostaff@bto.org
website: www.bto.org

The Wildlife Trusts
The Kiln
Waterside
Mather Road
Newark NG24 1WT
tel: (0870) 0367711
fax: (0870) 0360101
email: enquiry@wildlifetrusts.org
website: www.wildlifetrusts.org

Index

The page numbers in the index relate to all 184 species described in full in the 'species accounts' section. Cross-references can also be found in the 'identification' section.

Photography credits

Illustrations